THE LAW OF SPECIAL EDUCATION AND NON-PUBLIC SCHOOLS

Major Challenges in Meeting the Needs of Youth with Disabilities

Charles J. Russo, Allan G. Osborne Jr., Joseph D. Massucci, and Gerald M. Cattaro

Rowman & Littlefield Education
Lanham, Maryland • New York • Toronto • Plymouth, UK

Published in the United States of America
by Rowman & Littlefield Education
A Division of Rowman & Littlefield Publishers, Inc.
A wholly owned subsidiary of The Rowman & Littlefield Publishing Group, Inc.
4501 Forbes Boulevard, Suite 200, Lanham, Maryland 20706
www.rowmaneducation.com

Estover Road
Plymouth PL6 7PY
United Kingdom

British Library Cataloguing in Publication Information Available

Library of Congress Cataloging-in-Publication Data

Russo, Charles J., 1948–
The law of special education and non-public schools : major challenges in meeting the needs of youth with disabilities / Charles J. Russo . . . [et al.].
p. cm.
ISBN: 978-1-60709-238-4 (cloth : alk. paper)
ISBN: 978-1-60709-239-1 (pbk. : alk. paper)
ISBN: 978-1-60709-240-7 (e-book)
[etc.]
1. Special education—Law and legislation—United States. 2. Private schools—Law and
legislation —United States.
KF4220 .L39 2009
344.73/0791 22 2009004357

™ The paper used in this publication meets the minimum requirements of American National Standard for Information Sciences—Permanence of Paper for Printed Library Materials, ANSI/NISO Z39.48-1992.
Manufactured in the United States of America.

CONTENTS

Dedicated to Our Parents

James J. and Helen J. Russo
Allan G. and Ruth L. Osborne
Vincent James and Martha Ann Massucci
Vito and Lucy Cattaro

ACKNOWLEDGMENTS

We could not have written this book without the encouragement, support, advice, and assistance of many friends, colleagues, and family members. Even though it is impossible to acknowledge all who have influenced us in some way and so contributed to this book, we would at the very least like to extend our gratitude to those who have had the greatest impact in our lives. This group includes all who have contributed to our knowledge and understanding of the subject matter of this book, most notably our many friends and colleagues who are members of the Education Law Association. These professionals have not only consistently shared their knowledge with us but also, more importantly, provided constructive criticism and constantly challenged our thinking. We also include our graduate students in this book who, as educational practitioners, have kept us abreast of the problems they face daily in their schools.

We are also most fortunate to work with a group of professionals who understand the importance of our work and provide us with the support and resources to continue our research.

In the School of Education and Allied Professions at the University of Dayton, we, Charlie Russo and Fr. Joe Massucci, would like to express our thanks to Dr. Thomas J. Lasley Jr., Dean; and Dr. Dan Raisch, Associate Dean, for their ongoing support and friendship. I, Charlie, also extend a special note of thanks to my assistant Ms. Elizabeth Pearn for her valuable assistance in helping to process the manuscript and Ms.

Colleen Wildenhaus for her assistance in proofreading the final manuscript, as well as to Mrs. Ann Raney of the Curriculum Materials Center for the many times that she has helped me to find information for this book and many other projects.

Charlie Russo also extends a special note of thanks and appreciation to his two wonderful children, Emily Rebecca, David Peter, and his wife Li Hong. The bright and inquisitive children that my wife Debbie and I have been blessed with have grown to be wonderful young adults who provide us both with a constant source of inspiration and love.

Allan Osborne wishes to thank the staff, students, and parents of the Snug Harbor Community School in Quincy, Mass., for close to two and a half decades of rewards and inspiration. I also want to extend a big thank-you to my good friends and former colleagues, Dennis Carini and Carol Shiffer, and their respective spouses Peggy and Ed, for their support, encouragement, companionship, and friendship. A very special thank-you is extended to Dr. Phil DiMattia, my former mentor from Boston College, who first encouraged me to research legal issues in special education and, in particular, urged me to advocate for the rights of non-public school students with disabilities to receive a free appropriate public education.

A huge thank-you to Dr. Carmen Mariano, President of Archbishop Williams High School in Braintree, Mass., and former Assistant Superintendent of the Quincy Public Schools, for reviewing and commenting on an early draft of this book and for writing its foreword, from all four of us. His constructive criticism has helped us to make it more useful for non-public school administrators. More importantly, however, Carmen was a great friend and supporter to Allan during their years together in the Quincy Public Schools.

On behalf of Charlie and Allan, our wonderful wives, affectionately known as the two Debbies, have been the major influence in our lives and professional careers. Our best friends, they encourage us to write, show great patience as we ramble on endlessly about litigation in special education, and understand when we must spend countless hours working on a manuscript. We would not be able to do all that we do if it were not for their constant love and support.

Finally, we all extend our love and appreciation to our late parents, James J. and Helen J. Russo, Allan G. and Ruth L. Osborne, Vincent James and Martha Ann Massucci, and Vito and Lucy Cattaro. We can never adequately express our gratitude to our parents for the profound influences that they have had on our lives.

FOREWORD

My favorite movie stars Yul Brynner and Steve McQueen and was made in 1960. Its name? *The Magnificent Seven*.

In this magnificent movie, a team of seven gunfighters is hired by a small Mexican farming village to protect the citizens of the village from a band of forty-plus banditos led by an imposing villain named Calvera, who is played by Eli Wallach.

Things go well at first. The seven hired gunmen fight off the bandits in their first encounter and send them into the mountains that surround the village.

Alas, a villager turns traitor and helps Calvera and his men return to the village under cover of darkness and capture the seven defenders.

Rather than kill them, Calvera takes the weapons of the Magnificent Seven and orders them to return to the United States. As the seven leave the village, McQueen's character turns to Brynner and says, "I have no regrets. We owe them nothing. We never even signed anything. The only contract we had was in their hearts." Brynner's reply? "That is just the kind of contract you have to keep."

Moral? We do not owe each other that which is *legal*. We owe each other that which is *right*.

Thus, if a school like mine is served by nonunion teachers, those teachers deserve to be treated better than any union contract would demand. A contract only mandates what is legal. Teachers deserve what is right.

Yes, you know where I am going. As the president of a non-public, Catholic, coeducational, college preparatory high school, I may or may not have a *legal* obligation to recognize, accept, or accommodate the "special needs" of every student. Still, the word Catholic means *universal*. Thus, I have a *righteous* obligation to find the needs of each student, celebrate those needs, and address those needs within the means of my school's climate, culture, facilities, and finances.

It is therefore right for our teachers to serve small classes. It is also right for the levels at which our classes are taught to expand. College preparatory (CP), honors, and advanced placement (AP) classes are normal, but not enough. Accelerated classes, which serve students who require more of a challenge than CP classes provide but who are not yet ready for the rigor that honors classes bring, are offered as well.

Does any of that mean to imply that my school offers special education as it is legally defined by state or federal legislation? No, it does not. In fact, students who apply to Archbishop Williams High School (AWHS) are asked if they have individualized education programs (IEPs). Every candidate answering yes is advised to "enter with caution." They are told that we may not have the services required to properly serve them. That is hard for us to say. It is also not universal, and often untrue.

I once offered that same "enter with caution" message to a young man who came to a college I served. He was led by a dog, and had no eyes. That "told" me he had no hope of success in my school. I shared the message with that candidate. He enrolled anyway, and made his way to graduation as the class valedictorian.

Like that student, some of AWHS's "special needs" candidates apply despite our cautions. If accepted, they do not visit a resource room, or receive the kind of special services they would as public school students. Still, many of them succeed; on the strength of their spirit, the help of their teachers, and the sense of their self.

So what is my message? Just that special students are alive and well in our school, and we have a righteous obligation to offer them a special education. The law might not be satisfied with our efforts. It might require more. That will not change our mission or weaken our resolve. We will do our best to do what is *right*. We will continue to live with the spirit of the law in our hearts.

And we are not alone. Non-public schools everywhere embrace the same commitments, challenges, and choices that we do. None of us lacks passion. Still, until now, all of us have lacked direction. We looked in public school legislation for answers to non-public school questions. This book will change that. It breaks new ground for me and for non-public schools like mine. Never before have we (or any other non-public school) been guided by experts in public school special education law. I thank those experts and I welcome this book.

It has been said that "teachers save the world; one student at a time." This book will save the world; one private school at a time.

Carmen Mariano, EdD
President, Archbishop Williams High School
Braintree, Massachusetts

1

INTRODUCTION AND OVERVIEW

In the years following the enactment of Section 504 of the Rehabilitation Act of 1973 (Section 504)[1] and the 1975 adoption of the then Education for All Handicapped Children's Act, now the Individuals with Disabilities Education Act (IDEA),[2] the population of children in need of special education and related services has grown dramatically.[3] Not surprisingly, as the number of students who qualified for special education in public schools increased, so, too, did the number of children with special needs whose parents sought to have them educated in non-public schools, particularly those that were religiously affiliated.[4]

As perhaps the most explicit statement of support for students with disabilities from religious leaders in the United States, in their 1972 landmark statement, *To Teach as Jesus Did*, the American Catholic Bishops acknowledged that "[t]he right of the handicapped to receive religious education adapted to their special needs also challenges the ingenuity and commitment of the Catholic community."[5]

The American Catholic Bishops reaffirmed the principles of *To Teach as Jesus Did* in *In Support of Catholic Elementary and Secondary Schools* in 1990, and in 1998 the Bishops weighed in with *Welcome and Justice for Persons with Disabilities*.[6] Even in primarily addressing religious education outside of the regular programs in Catholic elementary and secondary schools, the Bishops presciently recognized, and sought to take steps to meet, the needs of the disabled.[7]

Regardless of a school's religious affiliation, or lack thereof, major challenges face educational leaders in non-public schools as they seek to meet the needs of growing numbers of parents[8] who wish to provide their children with disabilities with the benefits of education in non-public school settings. This challenge is exacerbated particularly in schools that are religiously affiliated, but may not be much less of a problem in schools that are nonsectarian, due to financial and constitutional constraints on their ability to provide services.

Even in the absence of clear data on the number of parents who wish to have their children with disabilities attend religiously affiliated and other types of non-public schools, including nonsectarian schools that largely provide special education,[9] the data reveal that significant numbers of students with such needs. For example, the most recent data from the National Center for Educational Statistics reveal that 42.7 percent of all non-public schools enrolled students with disabilities who had individualized education programs (IEPs).[10] While the 4 percent of children with IEPs in the total population of non-public schools dwarfed in comparison to the almost 14 percent of students in public schools, this statistic reveals that significant numbers of children in these schools are in need of special education and related services.

As educational leaders in non-public schools seek to address the schooling needs of children with disabilities, they can easily find themselves on the horns of a dilemma. On the one hand is the desire of religiously affiliated non-public schools to satisfy parents by meeting the educational needs of their children. On the other hand is the realistic challenge of seeking to pay what can be the significant costs associated with providing educational services for children with special needs who attend non-public schools, particularly because these schools primarily serve low- and middle-income families that cannot afford to pay much in the way of additional costs.

Cost issues associated with the delivery of special education are further complicated in light of provisions in the IDEA and its regulations, coupled with judicial interpretations of these provisions that place limits on how much public school boards are required to spend on students whose parents choose to enroll their children in religiously affiliated non-public schools. Educational leaders in non-public schools have justifiable reasons for concern that offering special education programs may impact significantly not only on schools and the majority of their students who are not disabled, but also on their budgets and those of their churches and related organizations that underwrite financial support. The situation is complicated by virtue of the fact that, moral considerations aside, religiously affiliated and other non-public schools are not legally obligated to accept children with disabilities.[11]

Even though religiously affiliated and other non-public schools are not legally bound to accept students with disabilities, it would be consistent with religious teachings, let alone basic human rights, to do so.[12] Additionally, non-public schools that serve students with disabilities make powerful statements backing up their espoused beliefs by making their schools more accessible to children with special needs. Consequently, it is important for educators, and all others who are interested in non-public schools, to be well acquainted with broad-based statutory rights of children with disabilities, most notably Section 504 and the IDEA, especially since these laws, like virtually all matters legal, continue to evolve.

It is particularly important for educators in non-public schools to have an awareness and understanding of Section 504, the IDEA, and other relevant statutes, because even if these laws do not always directly apply in non-public schools, parents who wish to place their children in these schools are increasingly knowledgeable about the statutory entitlements that their young might have received had they attended public schools. Many parents also have growing understanding of the extent to which some of the services under Section 504 and the IDEA might be available to their children who attend non-public schools.

When dealing with the IDEA and Section 504, Section 504 is more far-reaching since it covers students, staff, and even visitors in schools and at school activities (as well as at other places); even so, this book focuses on how Section 504 impacts the rights of students. The IDEA, on the other hand, is designed to provide a free appropriate public education to all students with disabilities in the least restrictive environment. Subject to its defense provisions, Section 504 applies to students in public and generally in non-public schools even though it does not provide financial assistance to school officials as they must develop policies and practices that comply with its dictates.

Conversely, while children with disabilities who are covered by the IDEA are occasionally enrolled in, and receive services at, non-public schools, this comprehensive statute has no direct application to students whose parents voluntarily enroll them in non-public schools since this law involves direct federal financial assistance. At the same time, nothing in federal law prevents states, through local school boards, from providing additional special education programs and services in non-public schools under their own laws.[13] To the extent that the IDEA places the obligation on the state, *qua* public schools, to ensure that each child with a disability receives a free appropriate public education,[14] all of those interested in non-public education, including religious and educational leaders, teachers, staff, parents, and interested members of supporting churches, will be well served to have a basic understanding of this complex statute and its regulations.

Insofar as Section 504 is not predicated on the direct receipt of federal assistance, in some circumstances it may apply to non-public schools.[15] Courts have ordinarily interpreted the qualification "recipient of financial assistance" in a fairly broad fashion that encompasses many private schools that may be the indirect recipients of federal funding.[16]

A case from Pennsylvania that also involved the Americans with Disabilities Act (ADA) reached the opposite result on the meaning of federal financial assistance under Section 504 as it applied to a religiously affiliated non-public school.[17] A student who was defiant in class, punched other children, and threatened other students was not readmitted to his religiously affiliated non-public school. After the student was diagnosed as having attention deficit hyperactivity disorder (ADHD), his father unsuccessfully filed suit claiming that the school refused to reenroll his son due to his disability. In granting the school's motion for summary judgment, the court determined that since the religious school was not a recipient of federal funds, it was not subject to Section 504. The court maintained that the fact that one student at the school received a free lunch was insufficient to alter its judgment. As a religious entity, the court added that the school was exempt from the ADA. The court concluded that the student was not substantially limited in the major life activity of learning because he earned grades at or near the top of his class and did not exhibit any difficulty with learning, and his father offered no authority to suggest that the student was impaired in his ability to concentrate or behave himself in class.

In this respect, Section 504 prohibits discrimination in private schools that accept students with disabilities by requiring educators to make individualized accommodations for children who are otherwise qualified. This means that all schools, including private schools that enroll students pursuant to Section 504, may have to provide aid, benefits, and/or services that are comparable to those available to students who do not have disabilities. Under these provisions, children with disabilities must receive comparable materials, teacher quality, length of school term, and daily hours of instruction.[18]

In like fashion, another far-reaching antidiscrimination statute that protects the rights of individuals with disabilities, the Americans with Disabilities Act,[19] applies to private schools except for those that are affiliated with religious entities.[20] Needless to say, this is a major exception that impacts a significant number of students and their families.

Given the legal issues surrounding the delivery of special education to children who attend non-public schools, this book is divided into six chapters.[21] This brief chapter sets the stage for the remainder of the book. Chapter 2 includes a brief overview of the legal system. Chapter 3 offers a brief history of equal educational opportunities before focusing on the rights of students with disabilities pursuant to Section 504 of the Rehabilitation Act of 1973. Chapter 4 examines the IDEA broadly in order to give readers a basic working understanding of this far-reaching law. Chapter 5 focuses on recent changes in the statute and implementing regulations as they apply to non-public schools along with issues in need of further clarification concerning the delivery of special education to children who attend non-public schools. Chapter 6 offers practical considerations for educators in non-public elementary and secondary schools as they think about implementing special education programs. The authors fervently hope that this book will provide interested readers with a better understanding of the relevant statutes, regulations, and cases that will assist them in their quest to better provide for the delivery of special education to children who attend non-public schools.

As an introductory matter, it is worth noting that the IDEA and its regulations actually use the terms *private* and *parochial* rather than *non-public* schools. However, insofar as religiously affiliated non-public schools are sufficiently different from and face different legal issues from schools that are not religiously affiliated, unless otherwise noted by the context, the authors use the terms *non-public* or *religiously affiliated non-public* schools when discussing these schools and private when dealing with schools that are nonsectarian or secular.

NOTES

1. 29 U.S.C.A. § 794. A third statute, the Americans with Disabilities Act (ADA), although noted later in this introduction, which is similar to Section 504, is largely beyond the scope of this book because it specifically exempts religious institutions from the scope of its coverage. The ADA, 42 U.S.C.A. §§ 12101 *et seq.*, was adopted in 1990 to provide "a comprehensive national mandate for the elimination of discrimination against individuals with disabilities." 42 U.S.C.A. § 12101(b)(2). In an area primarily dealing with employment, the ADA now essentially extends the protections of Section 504 to the private sector but has implications for public entities such as schools. Congress recently enacted the ADA Amendments Act of 2008, PL 110-325, 122 Stat. 3553, broadening the definition of disability, making it easier for individuals to prove that they were victims of workplace discrimination, especially those who suffered from epilepsy, diabetes, cancer, multiple sclerosis, and other ailments and who were improperly denied protection insofar as their conditions could be controlled by medications or other measures. The Act specifically exempts employers who may consider the mitigating effects of ordinary eyeglasses or contact lenses in evaluating whether visual impairments substantially limit major life activities. The ADA also modifies Section 504 so that the definitions of disability and major life activities in both laws are identical.
2. 20 U.S.C.A. §§ 1400 *et seq*. For the sake of consistency, this book refers to the IDEA throughout, even for cases that were resolved before its name change in 1990.
3. According to the United States Department of Education, the 8.3 percent of public school students who were served under the IDEA during the 1976–1977 school year, the first one reported in the table, rose to 12 percent during the 1993–1994 school year and 13.6 percent during the 2006–2007 year, the last year for which data are available. *The Condition of Education*, U.S. Department of Education, Washington, DC, 2008. Appendix 1. Supplemental Tables (Children and Youth with Disabilities in Public Schools).
4. As of the 2003–2004 academic year, 4.0 percent of all students enrolled in non-public schools had individualized education programs (IEPs). U.S. Department of Education, National Center for Educational Statistics, Schools and Staffing Survey, Private School Data File, Washington, DC (2008), p. 93.
5. *To Teach as Jesus Did: A Pastoral Message on Catholic Education* (1972).
6. Available at www.nccbuscc.org/doctrine/disabilities.htm.

7. *In Support of Catholic Elementary and Secondary Schools* (1990).

8. This book uses the term *parents* to include parents and guardians.

9. Some 2 percent of non-public schools are dedicated to providing special education exclusively to their students. *Characteristics of Private Schools in the United States: Results from the 2003–2004 Private School Universe Survey*, U.S. Department of Education, Institute of Education Sciences, NCES 2006, Washington, DC (2006), p. 19. For a discussion of some of these data, see Leonard DeFiore, "The State of Special Education in Catholic Schools," 9 *Catholic Education: A Journal of Inquiry and Practice* 453 (2001).

10. As of the 2003–2004 academic year, 4.0 percent of all students enrolled in non-public schools had IEPs. U.S. Department of Education, *National Center for Educational Statistics, Schools and Staffing Survey, Private School Data File* (Washington, D.C., 2008).

11. For discussions on the rights of children with disabilities who attend non-public schools, *see* Nikki L. Schweinbeck, "Section 504 and Catholic Schools," 4 *Catholic Education: A Journal of Inquiry and Practice* 464 (2001); Mary Elizabeth Blackett, "Recommendations for Catholic School Administrators in Facilitating Special Education Services," 4 *Catholic Education: A Journal of Inquiry and Practice* 479 (2001); Diana Lawrence-Brown and Kim. S. Muschaweck, "Getting Started with Collaborative Teamwork for Inclusion," 8 *Catholic Education: A Journal of Inquiry and Practice* 146 (2004); Rhomas J. Long and Merylann J. Schuttloffel, "A Rationale for Special Education in Catholic Schools," 9 *Catholic Education: A Journal of Inquiry and Practice* 443 (2006).

12. *See, e.g.*, *United Nations High Commission for Human Rights, Convention on the Rights of the Child* (1989): Article 23:

1. States Parties recognize that a mentally or physically disabled child should enjoy a full and decent life, in conditions which ensure dignity, promote self-reliance and facilitate the child's active participation in the community.
2. States Parties recognize the right of the disabled child to special care and shall encourage and ensure the extension, subject to available resources, to the eligible child and those responsible for his or her care, of assistance for which application is made and which is appropriate to the child's condition and to the circumstances of the parents or others caring for the child.
3. Recognizing the special needs of a disabled child, assistance extended in accordance with paragraph 2 of the present article shall be provided free of charge, whenever possible, taking into account the financial resources of the parents or others caring for the child, and shall be designed to ensure that the disabled child has effective access to and receives education, training, health care services, rehabilitation services, preparation for employment and recreation opportunities in a manner conducive to the child's achieving the fullest possible social integration and individual development, including his or her cultural and spiritual development.

13. 34 C.F.R. § 300.133(d).

14. 20 U.S.C.A. § 1411(a)(1).

15. 34 C.F.R. § 104.39.

16. *See, e.g.*, *Bob Jones Univ. v. United States*, 461 U.S. 574 (1983); *Hunt v. St. Peter Sch.*, 963 F. Supp. 843 (W.D. Mo. 1997).

17. *Marshall v. Sisters of the Holy Family of Nazareth*, 399 F. Supp.2d 597 (E.D. Pa. 2005).

18. Charles J. Russo and Allan G. Osborne Jr., *Section 504 and the ADA* (Thousand Oaks, CA: Corwin Press, 2009).

19. 42 U.S.C.A. §§ 12101 *et seq.* as amended by the ADA Amendments Act of 2008, P.L. 110-325, 122 Stat. 3553.

20. *Doe v. Abington Friends School*, 480 F.3d 252 (3d Cir. 2007); *White v. Denver Seminary*, 157 F. Supp.2d 1171 (D. Colo. 2001).

21. For earlier versions of some of the materials discussed herein, *see* Charles J. Russo and Allan G. Osborne Jr., "The Legal Rights of American Students with Disabilities: An Overview," 3 *Australia & New Zealand Journal of Law & Education*, No. 2, 45, (1998). Charles J. Russo, Joseph D. Massucci, and Allan G. Osborne Jr., "The Delivery of Special Education Services in Catholic Schools: One Hand Gives, the Other Hand Takes Away," 3 *Catholic Education: A Journal of Inquiry and Practice* 375 (2000).

2

NON-PUBLIC SCHOOLS AND THE AMERICAN LEGAL SYSTEM

Given its breadth and impact on the lives of all Americans, it is important for readers to understand the legal framework under which educational institutions function in the United States before engaging in any discussion of legal issues that arise in non-public schools. The purpose of this chapter, then, is to familiarize readers with the sources and types of laws in the American legal system while providing information on how these laws affect the daily operations of non-public schools. The chapter also includes a brief section on legal resources and a primer on reading legal citations. The chapter ends with a brief overview of the major statutes governing the delivery of special education services to students with disabilities.

SOURCES OF LAW

There are essentially four sources of law in the United States: constitutions, statutes, regulations, and judicial decisions. Each of these sources of law exists at both the federal and state levels. A constitution is the fundamental law of a nation or state[1] while a statute is an act of the legislative body, or a law enacted by Congress or a state legislature.[2] All statutes must be in harmony with the constitutions within their jurisdiction. Officials in the agencies responsible for the execution and enforcement of the statutes frequently issue regulations or guidelines for implementation of the statutes. Regulations are more specific than the statutes they are designed to implement in that they provide guidelines, based on legislative intent, as to how the laws should work in practice. Finally, the numerous opinions issued by the courts interpreting the constitutions, statutes, and regulations comprise a large body of law known as case, judge-made, or common law. Case law provides additional insight into how constitutions, statutes, and regulations should be applied to fact-specific situations.

CONSTITUTIONS

As most grade school students know, the Constitution of the United States is the law of the land. All federal statutes and regulations, state constitutions, state laws and regulations, and ordinances of local governmental bodies are subject to the Constitution as it has been interpreted by the courts. Yet, only a few sections of the U.S. Constitution are involved in education-related lawsuits. The sections of the Constitution that impact most dramatically on the day-to-day operation of educational institutions, including non-public schools, are the amendments protecting individual rights, such as the First (primarily dealing with freedom of religion and speech), Fourth (mainly involving searches of students and educators), and Fourteenth (focusing largely on due process and equal protection under the law) Amendments. Correspondingly, state constitutions are the supreme law of their states with which all other state statutes, regulations, and ordinances must conform. State constitutions by and large deal with many of the same topics as their federal counterpart.

STATUTES AND REGULATIONS

Under the Tenth Amendment to the Constitution, education is a function that is reserved to the states.[3] Even so, Congress has the authority to enact laws under the general welfare clause of Article I, Section 8, by providing funds for purposes that it feels will serve the public good. For example, Congress has passed several statutes, such as Section 504 of the Rehabilitation Act[4] that subjects educational institutions that receive federal funds to its antidiscrimination provisions.

Federal statutes frequently provide funds to state and local governments conditioned on their acceptance of specific requirements for the use of the money. When states accept federal funds, officials in beneficiary programs are bound by whatever conditions Congress has attached to the legislation. However, when these funding statutes are challenged, federal courts must be convinced that those conditions are constitutional. The definition of what constitutes a program or activity receiving federal funds was expanded by Congress in 1987 to include "all of the operations of [an entity] any part of which is extended Federal financial assistance."[5] This broad definition is implicated in statutes prohibiting discrimination by "race, color or national origin,"[6] "sex,"[7] and "otherwise qualified handicapped individuals,"[8] categories that have become increasingly important in educational settings.

Regulations issued by administrative agencies, such as the federal and state Departments of Education, give the executive branch of government the means to implement statutes by carrying out their full effect. While statutes set broad legislative parameters, regulations, on the other hand, are more extensive in that they are essentially detailed rules on what is required to satisfy the requirements of the law. Regulations generally carry the full force of the law unless courts interpret them as conflicting with the legislation.

Most of the law affecting non-public schools comes from statutes enacted by state legislatures. While state legislatures are subject to the limitations of federal law and of state constitutions, they are relatively free to establish their own systems of education and may enact laws that control the operation of non-public schools. While states cannot prohibit non-public schools from operating[9] they do have the authority to regulate their activities.[10]

COMMON LAW

When conflicts inevitably arise, it is the responsibility of the courts to interpret the law. When no codified law exists, or if statutes or regulations are not clear, courts apply what is known as common law. Common law is principally judge-made law, meaning that the courts may adjust the law to new or changing circumstances. The collective decisions of the courts make up the body of common law. When disputes involve legislation, the courts' task is to uncover, as best they can, the intent of the legislative bodies that enacted the statutes in question. To the degree that judicial decrees establish precedent, they have considerable weight in terms of providing guidance on how statutes and regulations are to be applied to everyday situations.

JUDICIAL SYSTEMS

The federal court system has three levels, as do most state court systems. At the lowest level in the federal system are trial courts, officially known as district courts. Each state has at least one federal district court while geographically larger states, such as California, Texas, and New York, may have as many as four. District courts are the basic triers of fact in legal disputes in that they review evidence and render decisions based on the evidence presented by the parties to disputes. Depending on the situation, such as is the case in disputes involving the delivery of special education services, trial courts may review the record of any administrative hearings that have been held, hear additional evidence, and/or hear the testimony of witnesses.

Any party not satisfied with the decision of a trial court may appeal to the federal circuit court of appeals within which their state is located. For example, a decision issued by a federal trial court in Massachusetts would be appealed to the First Circuit, which, in addition to Massachusetts, consists of the states of Maine, New Hampshire, and Rhode Island along with the Commonwealth of Puerto Rico. There are thirteen federal judicial circuits in the United States: eleven numbered circuits, the District of Columbia Circuit, and a special circuit dealing with appeals from federal districts.

Any party not satisfied with the decision of a circuit court may appeal to the Supreme Court. In light of the high volume of cases that are appealed each year, the Supreme Court accepts less than 1 percent in which parties seek further review. Cases typically reach the Court in requests for a writ of certiorari, which literally means "to be informed of." When the Supreme Court agrees to hear an appeal it grants a writ of certiorari. At least four of the nine justices must vote to grant certiorari in order for a case to be reviewed.[11] Denying a writ of certiorari has the effect of leaving the lower court's decision unchanged.[12]

Each of the fifty states and various territories has a similar arrangement to the federal scheme except that the names of the courts vary. A majority of states also have three levels of courts: trial courts, intermediate appellate courts, and courts of last resort. It is important to pay attention to the names of state courts as they may vary from state to state. For example, we usually think of a supreme court as being the highest court. Yet in New York, the state trial court is known as the Supreme Court while the state's highest court is named the Court of Appeals.

The decisions of courts are binding only within their own geographic jurisdictions. In other words, a ruling of a federal trial court for New York is binding only in New York. The federal trial court in Connecticut might find a decision of a New York court persuasive, but is not bound by its order and may issue a contrary opinion in a case that involves factual similarities. On the other hand, a ruling of the Second Circuit Court of Appeals would be binding on all states within its jurisdiction such that lower courts in New York, Connecticut, and Vermont must follow its precedent unless they can distinguish the facts a way to allow them to reach different outcomes. A decision by the Supreme Court of the United States is, of course, enforceable in all fifty states and American territories and becomes the law of the land.

As noted, the American judiciary operates at both the federal and state levels. The most widespread organization of these systems is a three-tiered structure of trial courts, intermediate appellate courts, and courts of last resort. Trial courts have general jurisdiction so that there are few constraints on the types of cases that they may hear. Trial courts review the facts behind the suit and apply the law to the circumstances. Trial courts are normally presided over by a single judge or justice. Intermediate level courts, which are commonly known as appellate courts or courts of appeal, review cases when parties are dissatisfied with the decisions of lower courts.

Appellate courts are not triers of fact. Instead, appellate courts review lower courts' application of the law. In rare cases, appellate courts may disregard findings of fact from lower courts if they are convinced that they were clearly erroneous. Appellate courts typically consist of a panel of judges. For example, at the federal level and in many state court systems appeals are heard by a panel of three judges. Finally, issues may be appealed to a court of last resort. At the federal level this is the Supreme Court. The Supreme Court has discretion to review rulings of lower federal courts and state high courts that involve federal constitutional, statutory, or regulatory issues.

To the extent that education is a state function and federal courts deal with disputes involving federal questions, most educational suits are decided by state courts. Unless they raise substantial federal questions, cases must be tried in state courts. If substantial federal questions are involved with state questions, disputes may be litigated in either state or federal courts. When federal courts examine cases involving both state and federal law, they must follow prior interpretations of state law made by the state courts within which they sit.

LEGAL RESOURCES

The written opinions of most courts are generally available in a variety of published formats. The official version of Supreme Court decisions are published in the *United States Reports*, abbreviated U.S. The same opinions, with additional research aids, are published in the *Supreme Court Reporter* (S. Ct.) and the *Lawyer's Edition*, now in its second series (L. Ed.2d). Judgments issued by the federal circuit courts of appeal can be found in the *Federal Reporter*, now in its third series (F.3d), while federal district court decisions are published in the *Federal Supplement*, now in its second series (F. Supp.2d).

State court decisions are published in a variety of sources, most notably West's National Reporter system, which divides the country up into seven regions: Atlantic, Northeastern, Northwestern, Pacific, South Eastern, Southwestern, and Southern. Most education-related cases are also republished in West's *Education Law Reporter*. Prior to being published in hardbound volumes, decisions are usually released in what are known as slip opinions, a variety of loose-leaf services, and electronic sources. There are also many commercial services available that publish decisions in a specialized area. For example, special education court decisions, as well as due process hearing decisions, are reproduced in a loose-leaf format in the *Individuals with Disabilities Education Law Reporter* (IDELR) published by LRP Publications.

Statutes and regulations are also available in similar formats. Federal statutes are located in the *United States Code* (U.S.C.), the official version, or the *United States Code Annotated* (U.S.C.A.), published by West Publishing Co. Agency regulations are officially published in the *Code of Federal Regulations* (C.F.R.). Copies of education statutes and regulations can be downloaded via links on the U.S. Department of Education's Web site. Legal materials are also available online from a variety of sources, such as WestLaw and LexisNexis. State laws and regulations are commonly available online from the Web sites of their state governments.

READING AND UNDERSTANDING LEGAL CITATIONS

Legal citations are not difficult to read. The first numeral in a citation indicates the volume number where the case, statute, or regulation is located followed by the abbreviation of the book or series in which the material is located. The second number indicates the page on which a case begins or the section number of a statute or regulation. The final part of a citation for a court opinion includes the name of the court, for lower court cases, and the year in which the dispute was resolved. For example, the citation for *Shapiro v. New York City Department of Education*, 561 F. Supp.2d 413 (S.D.N.Y. 2008) can be located in volume 561 of the Federal Supplement Second Series beginning on page 413. The case was decided by the District Court for the Southern District of New York in 2008. Similarly, the citation for the Individuals with Disabilities Education Act, 20 U.S.C.[A.] § 1400 *et seq*. (2005) can be found in volume 20 of the United States Code beginning with section 1400; the statute actually continues through section 1482.

LAWS GOVERNING SPECIAL EDUCATION

Special education in the United States is governed by four major federal laws: the Individuals with Disabilities Education Act (IDEA),[13] Section

504 of the Rehabilitation Act (Section 504),[14] the Americans with Disabilities Act (ADA),[15] and the No Child Left Behind Act (NCLB).[16] In addition each of the fifty states and U.S. territories has laws of their own governing special education. Each of these federal laws is discussed in greater detail later in this book.

SECTION 504 OF THE REHABILITATION ACT OF 1973

The Rehabilitation Act of 1973 was the first federal civil rights law designed to protect the rights of individuals with disabilities. Section 504 of that statute states that "[n]o otherwise qualified individual with a disability in the United States . . . shall, solely by reason of her or his disability, be excluded from the participation in, be denied the benefits of, or be subjected to discrimination under any program or activity receiving [f]ederal financial assistance."[17]

Section 504 applies to all institutions that receive "federal financial assistance." Thus, it applies to virtually all public and many, if not the vast majority of, non-public schools because this term has been interpreted broadly by the courts.[18] Thus, any non-public schools that are either the direct or indirect recipients of federal funding for any purpose (i.e., for lunch subsidies or health-related services) may come under the umbrella of Section 504. Further, Section 504 offers broad-based protection to individuals under the more nebulous concept of impairment rather than disability. Section 504 covers not only children, but also employees, and others who may visit an educational institution.

Once they have been identified as having disabilities, otherwise qualified students are entitled to an appropriate public education, regardless of the nature or severity of their impairments. To guarantee that an appropriate education is provided, Section 504's regulations include due process requirements for evaluation and placement similar to, but not nearly as extensive as, those under the IDEA.[19] In making accommodations for students with disabilities, school personnel must provide aid, benefits, and/or services that are comparable to those available to children who do not have impairments. Thus, otherwise qualified students must receive comparable materials, teacher quality, length of school term, and daily hours of instruction. Additionally, programs for qualified students should not be separate from those available to students who do not have disabilities unless such segregation is necessary for their educational programming to be effective. While schools are not prohibited from offering separate programs for students who have impairments, these children cannot be required to attend such classes unless they cannot be served adequately in more inclusive settings.[20] When such programs are offered separately, facilities must, of course, be comparable to those available to students who do not have disabilities.[21]

Section 504's only regulation directly addressing non-public schools declares that officials in such schools may not exclude students on the basis of their conditions if they can, with minor adjustments, be provided with appropriate educations.[22] Further, this regulation specifies that non-public schools "may not charge more for the provision of an appropriate education to handicapped persons than to nonhandicapped persons except to the extent that any additional charge is justified by a substantial increase in cost to the recipient."[23] As such, non-public schools may be able to charge additional costs to parents of children with impairments.

AMERICANS WITH DISABILITIES ACT

The Americans with Disabilities Act (ADA),[24] enacted in 1990, protects individuals with disabilities by imposing extensive obligations on private sector employers, public services and accommodations, and transportation. As explained in its preamble, the purpose of the ADA, which was modeled on Section 504, is "to provide a clear and comprehensive national mandate for the elimination of discrimination against individuals with disabilities."[25] This statement makes it clear that the ADA was intended to extend the protections granted by Section 504 to private programs and activities that are not covered by the latter statute because they do not receive federal funds.

The ADA is a comprehensive federal mandate designed to eliminate discrimination against people with disabilities by imparting "clear, strong, consistent and enforceable standards"[26] to help achieve this goal. The ADA's broad definition of a disability is practically identical to the one in Section 504.[27] Further, many other definitions in the ADA are analogous to the equivalent definitions in Section 504. The ADA, similar to Section 504, does not require that individuals have certificates from doctors or psychologists to be covered by its provisions.

The ADA specifically excludes a variety of individuals, few of whom are apt to be students but some may be school employees. Excluded from the ADA's protections are those who use illegal drugs;[28] transvestites;[29] homosexuals and bisexuals;[30] transsexuals, pedophiles, exhibitionists, voyeurs, and those with sexual behavior disorders;[31] and individuals with conditions such as psychoactive substance use disorders stemming from current illegal use of drugs.[32] The ADA modifies Section 504 to the extent that it covers individuals who are no longer engaged in illegal drug use, including those who have successfully completed drug treatment or have otherwise been rehabilitated and those who have been "erroneously" regarded as being drug users.[33] The ADA allows employers to conduct drug tests to ensure that workers are in compliance with the Drug-Free Workplace Act of 1988.[34] Interestingly, even though the ADA permits employers to prohibit the use of illegal drugs or alcohol in the workplace, it is less clear over the status of alcoholics, but it does appear that the protections given to rehabilitated drug users extend to recovering alcoholics.

The ADA has five major Titles. Title I speaks to employment in the private sector and is directly applicable to non-public schools. As with Section 504, Title I requires school officials to make reasonable accommodations for otherwise qualified individuals once officials are aware of the individuals' conditions. This means that to be covered by the ADA, students and employees must inform school officials of their conditions along with specific suggestions on how their needs can be accommodated. Title II covers public services of state and local governments for both employers and providers of public services, including transportation and as such does not directly apply to non-public schools. Insofar as the reasonable accommodations specifications in these provisions suggest academic program accommodations, qualified students with disabilities must be allowed to participate in school activities.

Title III of the ADA expands the scope of Section 504 by addressing places of public accommodation in both the private and public sectors. This Title includes private entities and a wide array of community services, including buildings, transportation systems, parks, recreational facilities, hotels, and theaters. Title IV deals with telecommunications, specifically voice and nonvoice systems. In Title V, which includes the ADA's miscellaneous provisions, the statute stipulates not only that the law cannot be construed as applying a lesser standard than that under Section 504 and its regulations but also that qualified individuals are not required to accept services that do not meet their needs.

The ADA's impact on non-public schools is most significant in the areas of reasonable accommodations for employees and academic program accommodations for students. Officials in non-public schools should designate ADA compliance officers who are responsible for keeping up to date on current ADA regulations and policies in the areas of employment and academic inclusion.

INDIVIDUALS WITH DISABILITIES EDUCATION ACT

In 1975 Congress enacted a statute that at that time was known as the Education for All Handicapped Children Act. In 1990 Congress amended this landmark legislation and in doing so gave the law its present title, the Individuals with Disabilities Act (IDEA). The IDEA underwent additional major changes in 1997 and again in 2004.

The IDEA requires states, and consequently school districts, to provide a free appropriate public education (FAPE) to all students with disabilities in the least restrictive environment.[35] Students with disabilities must meet three statutory requirements to receive services under the act: They must be between the ages of three and twenty-one;[36] they must have specifically identified disabilities;[37] and, they must be in need of special education,[38] meaning that they must require specially designed instruction to receive a FAPE[39] that conforms to an individualized education program (IEP).[40] Further, students with disabilities are entitled to receive related, or supportive, services, such as transportation, psychological services, physical therapy, and occupational therapy, to assist them in benefiting from their IEPs.[41]

A unique feature of the IDEA is that it contains an elaborate system of procedural safeguards to protect the rights of children and their parents.[42] Those procedures require school officials to provide written notice and obtain parental consent prior to evaluating students,[43] making initial placements, or initiating changes in placements.[44] In addition, the parents of students with disabilities must be given the opportunity to participate in the development of the IEPs for and placement of their children.[45] Once placed, the IEPs of all students must be reviewed at least annually[46] and students must be reevaluated at least once every three years unless their parents and local school officials agree that reevaluations are unnecessary.[47] Also, the IDEA has provisions, supplemented by the Family Educational Rights and Privacy Act[48] and its regulations,[49] which preserve the confidentiality of all information used in the evaluation, placement, and education of students.

As discussed throughout this book, non-public schools are not required to implement the IDEA's mandates. Even so, the IDEA does require local school boards to spend a proportionate share of their federal special education dollars on students who attend non-public schools. This aspect of the law is the subject of much of this book and is discussed in greater detail in subsequent chapters.

NO CHILD LEFT BEHIND ACT

Another important and controversial piece of federal legislation, the NCLB,[50] was enacted in 2002.[51] Although not directly applicable to non-public schools, the NCLB, which is actually an extension of the original Elementary and Secondary Education Act of 1965, has the potential to affect the delivery of special education services in all educational environments. It is also important for non-public school educators to understand the provisions of the NCLB, as it sets standards for achievement and accountability for public schools. Personnel in non-public schools need to be aware of these standards as they establish their own standards for a quality education.

The major provisions of the NCLB are intended to improve the academic achievement of students who are economically disadvantaged; assist in preparing, training, and recruiting highly qualified teachers; provide improved language instruction for children of limited English proficiency; make school systems accountable for student achievement, particularly by imposing standards for annual yearly progress for students and districts; require school systems to rely on teaching methods that are research based and that have been proven effective; and afford parents better choices while creating innovative educational programs, especially where local school systems are unresponsive to parents' needs.

NOTES

1. B. A. Garner, ed., *Black's Law Dictionary,* 8th ed. (Eagan, MN: West, 2004).
2. (Garner 2004).
3. *See Antonio Independent School District v. Rodriguez*, 411 U.S. 1, 35 (1973) ("Education, of course, is not among the rights afforded explicit protection under our Federal Constitution. Nor do we find any basis for saying it is implicitly so protected.").
4. 29 U.S.C.A. § 794.
5. Civil Rights Restoration Act, 20 U.S.C.A. § 1687.
6. 42 U.S.C.A. § 2000d.
7. 20 U.S.C.A. § 1681.
8. 29 U.S.C.A. § 794.
9. *Pierce v. Society of Sisters*, 268 U.S. 510 (1925).
10. Ralph D. Mawdsley, *Legal Problems of Religious and Private Schools*, 5th ed., (Dayton, OH: Education Law Association, 2006).
11. (Mawdsley 2006).
12. (Garner 2004).
13. 20 U.S.C.A. §§ 1400 *et seq.* (2005).
14. 29 U.S.C.A. § 794 (1973).
15. 42 U.S.C.A. § 12101 *et seq.* (1990).
16. 20 U.S.C.A. § 6301 *et seq.*
17. 29 U.S.C.A. § 794(a).
18. *Bob Jones Univ. v. United States*, 461 U.S. 574 (1983).
19. 34 C.F.R. § 104.36.
20. 34 C.F.R. § 104.4(b)(3).
21. 34 C.F.R. § 104.34(c).
22. 34 C.F.R. § 104.39(a).
23. 34 C.F.R. § 104.39(b).
24. 42 U.S.C.A. §§ 12101 *et seq.* as amended by the ADA Amendments Act of 2008, PL 110-325, 122 Stat. 3553.
25. 42 U.S.C.A. § 12101.
26. 42 U.S.C.A. § 12101(b)(2).
27. 42 U.S.C.A. § 12102(2).
28. 42 U.S.C.A. § 12210.
29. 42 U.S.C.A. § 12208.

30. 42 U.S.C.A. § 12211(a).
31. 42 U.S.C.A. § 12211(b).
32. 42 U.S.C.A. § 12211(c).
33. 42 U.S.C.A. § 12110.
34. 41 U.S.C.A. § 701.
35. 20 U.S.C.A. § 1412(5).
36. 20 U.S.C.A. § 1412(a)(1)(A).
37. 20 U.S.C.A. § 1401(3)(A)(i).
38. 20 U.S.C.A. § 1401(3)(A)(ii).
39. 20 U.S.C.A. § 1401(9).
40. 20 U.S.C.A. §§ 1401(14), 1414(d).
41. 20 U.S.C.A. § 1401(3)(A)(ii).
42. 20 U.S.C.A. § 1415.
43. 20 U.S.C.A. § 1414(a)(1)(d)(i)(I).
44. 20 U.S.C.A. § 1415(b)(3)(A).
45. 20 U.S.C.A. §§ 1414(d)(1)(B)(i), 1414(f).
46. 20 U.S.C.A. § 1414(d)(4).
47. 20 U.S.C.A. § 1414(a)(2)(A), (B)(ii).
48. 29 U.S.C.A. § 1232g.
49. 34 C.F.R. §§ 99.1 *et seq.*
50. 20 U.S.C.A. § 6301 *et seq.*
51. For a discussion of the NCLB, *see* C. Daniel Raisch and Charles J. Russo, "The No Child Left Behind Act: Federal Over-Reaching or Necessary Educational Reform?" 7 *Education Law Journal* (2006) 255.

3

SECTION 504 OF THE REHABILITATION ACT AND STUDENTS WITH DISABILITIES IN NON-PUBLIC SCHOOLS

Perhaps the most important case involving American non-public schools was *Pierce v. Society of Sisters* (*Pierce*),[1] wherein the Supreme Court ruled in favor of the proprietors of a Catholic school and a private military school. In the face of a statute that would have required parents to send their children to public schools as the only way to comply with Oregon's compulsory attendance law, the Court ruled that the law would have violated the Fourteenth Amendment to the United States Constitution because it would have denied the owners of the schools of their property of ownership rights. The Court conceded that although states may oversee such important features as health, safety, and teacher qualifications relating to the operation of non-public schools, they could not do so to an extent greater than they did for public schools. In practice, non-public schools are largely exempt from state requirements other than those dealing with health and safety.

Pierce is also important because it stands for the proposition that parents could satisfy a state's compulsory attendance law by sending their children to the non-public schools of their choice. *Pierce*, which can be considered a Magna Carta of sorts for parental rights, non-public schools, educational choice, and religious freedom, helped to ensure religious freedom in education by recognizing the right of non-public schools to operate. In the years since *Pierce*, non-public schools have undeniably contributed greatly to ensuring equal educational opportunities for millions of students throughout the United States.[2]

On a broader basis, the impetus for ensuring equal educational opportunities for all American children can be traced to *Brown v. Board of Education of Topeka* (*Brown*).[3] Although resolved in the context of school desegregation, in *Brown* the Supreme Court set the tone for later developments including those leading to protecting the rights of students with disabilities in its assertion that "[e]ducation is perhaps the most important function of state and local governments."[4]

In the years following *Brown*, an attitude of not always so benign neglect remained in effect with regard to the disabled. In fact, throughout the 1950s, twenty-eight states had laws requiring the sterilization of individuals with disabilities while others limited such basic rights as voting, marrying, and obtaining a driver's license.[5] By the 1960s, the percentages of children who were served in public schools began to rise; the 12 percent of children in public schools in 1948 increased to 21 percent in 1963 and 38 percent in 1968.[6] As of July 1, 1974, the Bureau for the Education of the Handicapped reported that about 78.5 percent of the nation's 8,150,000 eligible children with disabilities received some form of public education. Of these children, 47.8 percent received special education and related services, 30.7 percent did not receive related services, and the remaining 21.5 percent did not receive educational services at all.[7]

Statistical data aside, a major push for the development of special education came in two federal cases that set the stage for subsequent statutory developments. In *Pennsylvania Association for Retarded Children v. Pennsylvania* (*PARC*),[8] a federal trial court, in a consent decree, established the bases for what developed into the IDEA. In *PARC* the parties agreed that children with disabilities could neither be denied admission to a public school nor be subjected to a change in educational placement unless their parents received procedural due process and that a placement in a regular school classroom was preferable to one in a more restrictive setting. *PARC* also recognized that children can learn in a school setting.

Similarly, in *Mills v. Board of Education of the District of Columbia* (*Mills*),[9] a federal trial court ruled that despite the school system's claims that it lacked the resources for all of its students, it could not deny services to children with disabilities and that they could not be excluded from public schools without receiving due process. Since *Mills* was litigated in Washington, D.C., it was probably among the more significant influences moving federal lawmakers to act to ensure adequate protection for children with disabilities when they adopted Section 504 and the IDEA.

In light of legal developments following *PARC* and *Mills*, this chapter reviews major statutory developments under Section 504 aimed at safeguarding the educational rights of students with disabilities who attend non-public schools. In the wake of the literally thousands of suits that have been filed in federal and state courts, this chapter discusses selected cases under the appropriate headings rather than as separate entries.

SECTION 504 OF THE REHABILITATION ACT OF 1973

The Rehabilitation Act of 1973, part of a much older statute that traces its origins to World War I and provided assistance to soldiers who were injured in battle, was the first federal civil rights law protecting the rights of individuals who were disabled.[10] At its heart, Section 504 declares that "[n]o otherwise qualified individual with a disability in the United States . . . shall, solely by reason of her or his disability, be excluded from the participation in, be denied the benefits of, or be subjected to discrimination under any program or activity receiving [f]ederal financial assistance. . . . "[11]

This section briefly reviews the provisions of Section 504 applicable to students (and their parents) as they seek the benefits of the programs and services offered by non-public schools. When thinking of the far-reaching impact that Section 504 can have on schools, both financial and programmatic, New York City's former mayor Ed Koch's remark that it would have been easier for New York City to have purchased limousines for all individuals with disabilities than to pay to make its bus system fully accessible when the ADA was enacted comes to mind.[12] Hyperbole aside, since the ADA borrows heavily on the language of Section 504, a good argument can be made that if parents were better aware of the availability of Section 504 to access educational programming for their children, then schools would likely be significantly different places. With this in mind, this chapter lays the groundwork for the remainder of the book

Section 504, which is predicated on an institution's receipt of federal financial assistance,[13] is applicable to non-public schools[14] because this term is construed so broadly,[15] offers broad-based protection to individuals under the more amorphous concept of impairment rather than disability. It is important to note that while Section 504 covers students, employees, and others, this book focuses on the rights of children. Section 504 defines an individual with a disability as one "who (i) has a physical or mental impairment which substantially limits one or more of such person's major life activities, (ii) has a record of such an impairment, or (iii) is regarded as having such an impairment."[16]

In order to have a record of impairment, an individual must have a history of, or been identified as having, a mental or physical impairment that substantially limits one or more major life activities,[17] including schooling.[18] Once a student is identified as having a disability, the next step is to determine whether he or she is *otherwise qualified*. In order to be *otherwise qualified*, as the term is applied to preschool, elementary, and secondary school students, a child must be "(i) of an age during which nonhandicapped persons are provided such services, (ii) of any age during which it is mandatory under state law to provide such services to handicapped persons, or (iii) [a student] to whom a state is required to provide a free appropriate public education [under the IDEA]."[19] An individual who is *otherwise qualified*, meaning that he or she is eligible to participate in a program or activity despite the existence of an impairment, must be permitted to participate in the program or activity as long as it is possible to do so by means of a "reasonable accommodation."[20]

Reasonable accommodations may involve minor[21] adjustments such as permitting a child to be accompanied by a service dog,[22] modifying a behavior policy to accommodate a student with an autoimmune disease who was disruptive,[23] or providing a hearing interpreter for a student.[24] In a case from Minnesota, the federal trial court rejected a school board's motion for summary judgment that would essentially have dismissed the claim of parents who requested that officials provide training for staff members at a day care center to provide glucagon injections for a child with Type I diabetes.[25] The court thought that since the parents raised issues of fact about the reasonableness and burdensomeness of their request, it should have been permitted to proceed to trial on the merits of the claim.

In an interesting case dealing with discipline and a student with a learning disability who attended a Catholic high school, a federal trial court in Ohio rejected his claim that officials failed to make a reasonable accommodation when he was expelled for violating the school's drug policy.[26] Insofar as the court was satisfied that officials expelled the student for a legitimate nondisability based reason in light of his possession of marijuana on campus, his claim that he was denied a reasonable accommodation in not being able to remain in the school was without merit. Earlier, in a dispute from Missouri, a federal trial court decided that officials in a Catholic school did not violate Section 504 when they refused to maintain a mandatory "scent-free" environment for a child with severe asthma. The court was satisfied that insofar as the student was not otherwise qualified to participate in its educational program, the school's voluntary scent-free policy met Section 504's "minor adjustment" standard.[27]

Academic modifications usually include permitting children longer periods of time to complete examinations or assignments, using peer tutors, distributing outlines in advance, employing specialized curricular materials, and/or permitting students to use laptop computers to record answers on examinations. Yet, in a case that admittedly arose under the IDEA rather than Section 504, and in a public, rather than a non-public school, the Second Circuit was of the opinion that a student in New York with a learning disability could not use a more advanced calculator in a mathematics class since he was capable of passing the course without its use.[28] In reaching what would have been the same result under Section 504, the court explained that the student's own lack of effort led to his having failed and that having allowed him to use the calculator would have been inconsistent with the educational goals of the course.

In modifying facilities, school officials do not have to make every classroom and/or area of a building accessible. Rather, it may be enough to bring services to a child such as offering a keyboard for musical instruction rather than revamping an entire music room for a student who wishes to take piano classes.[29]

Even if a child appears to be "otherwise qualified," school officials can rely on one of three defenses to avoid being charged with noncompliance of Section 504. This represents a major difference between Section 504 and the IDEA since no such defenses are applicable under the latter.[30] Moreover, it is important to recognize that the courts generally defer to educational decision making in this arena.[31] First, schools can be excused from making accommodations that would result in "a fundamental alteration in the nature of [a] program."[32] The second defense permits school officials to avoid compliance if a modification imposes "undue financial burden[s]."[33]

The third defense is that an otherwise qualified student with a disability can be excluded from a program if his or her presence creates a substantial risk of injury to himself, herself, or others.[34] For example, a child with a spastic condition could possibly be excluded from a class that meets in a biology laboratory due to fears of being injured while working near the flames or a scalpel for use in dissecting animals. However, in order to comply with Section 504, school officials would probably have to offer a reasonable accommodation, such as providing a computer assisted program to accomplish an instructional goal similar to the one that would have been achieved in laboratory classes. Similarly, even though allowing students to use service dogs would normally be considered a reasonable accommodation, officials may not have to allow such a modification if they can demonstrate that the dogs would present a health risk to other students who may be allergic.[35]

Section 504 prohibits discrimination by requiring educators to make individualized modifications for otherwise qualified students with disabilities. This means that all schools, including non-public schools, assuming that they have admitted children pursuant to Section 504, must provide aid, benefits, and/or services that are comparable to those available to students who are not disabled. As such, children with disabilities must receive comparable materials, teacher quality, length of school term, and daily hours of instruction. These programs should not be separate from those available to students who do not have disabilities unless such segregation is necessary for the program to be effective.

While schools are not prohibited from offering separate programs for students with disabilities, children cannot be required to attend segregated classes unless they cannot be served adequately in a more inclusive setting.[36] If special programs are offered separately, facilities must, of course, be comparable.[37] If non-public schools offer special programs for students with disabilities, they may not charge more for such services "except to the extent that any additional charge is justified by a substantial increase in cost."[38] Of course, how much more schools can charge largely depends on how much families can afford to pay, often presenting parents with the draconian choice of affording their children the opportunity to be educated in the schools of their choice that may be unable to meet all of the educational needs of their young or to send them to schools that can provide the services but do not provide the religious ethos that they desire.

Once identified, all qualified students with disabilities are entitled to receive an appropriate public education, regardless of the nature or severity of their disabilities. In order to guarantee that an appropriate education is made available, Section 504's regulations include due process requirements for evaluation and placement similar to those under the IDEA.[39] Finally, Section 504, which is enforced by the Office of Civil Rights, requires all recipients of federal financial aid to file assurances of compliance; provide notice to students and their parents that their programs are nondiscriminatory; engage in remedial actions where violations are proven; take voluntary steps to overcome the effects of conditions that resulted in limiting the participation of students with disabilities in their programs; conduct a self-evaluation; designate a staff member, typically at the central office level, as compliance coordinator; and adopt grievance procedures.[40]

ADMISSIONS EXAMINATIONS/STANDARDS

In a related vein, it is worth keeping in mind that non-public schools in some parts of the United States, including those that consider admitting students with disabilities, require applicants to take admissions examinations and/or be interviewed prior to acceptance or placement[41] in order to determine whether they are otherwise qualified. In one such case, the First Circuit observed that an independent non-public school in Vermont was not required to admit a student who could not meet its requirement of performing at a fifth grade level since she was not otherwise qualified.[42]

In its analysis, the court noted that Section 504 does not require an educational institution to lower its standards.

Under Section 504, schools relying on examinations or interviews may be required to provide reasonable accommodations to applicants who have disabilities. While school officials are not required to alter the content of examinations or interviews, they may be required to make accommodations in how tests are administered or interviews are conducted. In other words, school officials would not be required to make examinations easier so that students who simply lacked the requisite knowledge could pass,[43] but they may have to alter the conditions under which examinations are administered, or interviews are conducted, so that students with disabilities with the requisite knowledge and skills to pass or express themselves fully can do so in spite of their disabilities.

Accommodations for examinations may be as simple as providing quiet rooms without distractions, essentially private rooms away from others, for students who suffer from attention deficit hyperactivity disorder or procuring the services of readers or braille versions of examinations for applicants who are sight-impaired. Further, students with physical challenges may require special seating arrangements, scribes to record answers to questions, and/or be permitted to use laptop or desktop computers to record answers on examinations. Similarly, whether as part of examinations or admissions interviews, students who are hearing impaired might be entitled to the services of sign-language interpreters to communicate directions that are normally given orally. At the same time, school officials may be required to provide students with learning disabilities with extra time in which to complete examinations or make computers available to children who may be more comfortable with them than with traditional paper and pencil tests.

Prior to receiving accommodations, students and their parents may have to prove that they have impairments, such as being learning disabled[44] and that, for example, the extra time they need to complete examinations is necessary due to their conditions.[45] Again, the purpose of providing the extra time would be to allow students, who might have difficulty processing information, sufficient opportunity to show that they are capable of answering the questions.

As noted, it is the responsibility of students and their parents to make school officials aware of the fact that they have disabilities and need accommodations in testing or interviewing. To this end, principals and other school officials should require proof that students have disabilities in need of accommodations in order for them to demonstrate knowledge and skills on the examination. Students, through their parents, should also suggest which accommodations would be most appropriate. In considering whether students are entitled to accommodations, school officials must make individualized inquiries. School officials would violate Section 504 if they refused to make testing accommodations or made modifications only for students with certain specified disabilities.

SECTION 504 SERVICE PLANS

Students who qualify under the Section 504 definition are entitled to reasonable accommodations so that they may access a school's programs. Making accommodations may involve alterations to the physical plant, such as building wheelchair ramps or removing architectural barriers, so that students may physically enter and get around the school building.[46] Under most circumstances schools must also allow students to bring service dogs into the classroom.[47] School officials are not required to provide accommodations that go beyond what would be considered to be reasonable. As noted under the defense to Section 504, accommodations that are excessively expensive, expose the school's staff to excessive risk, or that require a school to substantially modify the mission or purpose of a program would not be required.[48]

Although not specifically required by Section 504, many schools spell out the accommodations and services that will be provided to an eligible student in a written service plan. Since written service plans are not mandated by federal law, the components of service plans are likewise not mandated. In fact, the term that is commonly used, *Section 504 plans,* is nowhere in federal law. Even so, school officials should develop written service plans since they provide proof that educators responded to student needs and helped to avoid misunderstandings as to exactly what accommodations were to have been provided. In practical terms, Section 504 services plans should, at a minimum, include the following components:

Demographic Data Student's name, date of birth, school identification number, grade, school, teacher, parents' names, address, telephone numbers, and the like;

Team Members A listing of all team members, and their respective roles, who contributed to the development of the service plan;

Disability A description of the student's disability, and its severity, along with an explanation of how it impedes the child's educational progress; and

Accommodations and Services A detailed description of the accommodations and services to be offered under the plan, including the frequency and location of services and where they will be provided.

In addition, plans should also attach evaluative reports or assessments that helped to determine the nature of students' disabilities and the need for accommodations and services.

NOTES

1. 268 U.S. 510 (1925).

2. The Supreme Court recognized the contributions of non-public schools in *Board of Education v. Allen*, 392 U.S. 236, 247-48 (1968) (upholding a statute from New York that required local school boards to loan textbooks for secular instruction to all students regardless of where they attended school: "private education has played and is playing a significant and valuable role in raising national levels of knowledge, competence, and experience. Americans care about the quality of the secular education available to their children. They have considered high quality education to be an indispensable ingredient for achieving the kind of nation, and the kind of citizenry, that they have desired to create. Considering this attitude, the continued willingness to rely on private school systems, including parochial systems, strongly suggests that a wide segment of informed opinion, legislative and otherwise, has found that those schools do an acceptable job of providing secular education to their students. This judgment is further evidence that parochial schools are performing, in addition to their sectarian function, the task of secular education.").

3. 347 U.S. 483 (1954).

4. 347 U.S. 493.

5. Stephen B. Thomas and Charles J. Russo, *Special Education: Issues and Implications for the '90s* (1995) at 4–5. *See also* Allan G. Osborne Jr., *Legal Issues in Special Education* (1996) at 3–4.

6. Joseph Ballard, Bruce A. Ramirez, and Frederick J. Weintraub, *Special Education in America: Its Legal and Governmental Foundations* (1982) at 2.

7. House Report No. 332, 94th Congress (1975) at 11.

8. 334 F. Supp. 1257 (E.D. Pa. 1971), 343 F. Supp. 279 (E.D. Pa. 1972).

9. 348 F. Supp. 866 (D.D.C. 1972).

10. Richard K. Scotch, *From Good Will to Civil Rights: Transforming Federal Disability Policy* (Philadelphia: Temple University Press, 2001).

11. 29 U.S.C.A. § 794(a). For a lengthier discussion of this topic, *see* Charles J. Russo and Allan G. Osborne Jr., *Section 504 and the ADA* (Thousand Oaks, CA: Corwin Press, 2009).

12. Martin Bricketto (2003 April 21). Transportation as civil rights for the disabled. *Gotham Gazette*, available at www.gothamgazette.com/article //20030421/202/355 (last accessed October 20, 2008).

13. In an interesting case, a federal trial court in Louisiana rejected the argument of a Catholic school and the diocese, that while the school received federal financial assistance, it was not a recipient within the meaning of Section 504. As such, the court permitted parental claim that school officials failed to accommodate their son's disability, attention deficit hyperactivity disorder, to proceed. *Dupre v. Roman Catholic Diocese of Houma-Thibodaux*, 1999 WL 694081 (E.D. La. 1999).

14. 34 C.F.R. § 104.39 Private education.

> (a) A recipient that provides private elementary or secondary education may not, on the basis of handicap, exclude a qualified handicapped person if the person can, with minor adjustments, be provided an appropriate education, as defined in § 104.33(b)(1), within that recipient's program or activity.
>
> (b) A recipient to which this section applies may not charge more for the provision of an appropriate education to handicapped persons than to nonhandicapped persons except to the extent that any additional charge is justified by a substantial increase in cost to the recipient.
>
> (c) A recipient to which this section applies that provides special education shall do so in accordance with the provisions of §§ 104.35 and 104.36. Each recipient to which this section applies is subject to the provisions of §§ 104.34, 104.37, and 104.38.

15. *See Bob Jones Univ. v. United States*, 461 U.S. 574 (1983) (upholding the revocation of tax exempt status on the ground that it constitutes federal financial assistance). *See also Hunt v. St. Peter School*, 26 IDELR 6 (W.D. Mo. 1997) (directing a Catholic school to comply with Section 504 because it received federal funds through Title I and other federal programs).

16. 29 U.S.C.A. § 706(7)(B). The regulations further define physical or mental impairments as including:

> (A) any physiological disorder or condition, cosmetic disfigurement, or anatomical loss affecting one or more of the following body systems: neurological; musculoskeletal; special

sense organs; respiratory, including speech organs; cardiovascular; reproductive, digestive, genito-urinary; hemic and lymphatic; skin; and endocrine; or

(B) any mental or psychological disorder, such as mental retardation, organic brain syndrome, emotional or mental illness, and specific learning disorders. 34 C.F.R. § 104(j)(2)(I). Further, a note accompanying this list indicates that it merely provides examples of the types of impairments that are covered; it is not meant to be exhaustive.

17. An individual who is regarded as having an impairment has:

(A) a physical or mental impairment that does not substantially limit major life activities but that is treated by a recipient as constituting such a limitation; (B) a physical or mental impairment that substantially limits major life activities only as a result of the attitudes of others toward such impairment; or (C) none of the impairments . . . but is treated by a recipient as having such an impairment. 34 C.F.R. § 104.3(j)(2)(iv).

18. According to the regulations, "'Major life activities' means functions such as caring for one's self, performing manual tasks, walking, seeing, hearing, speaking, breathing, learning, and working." 34 C.F.R. § 104.3(j)(2)(I).

19. 45 C.F.R. § 104.3(k)(2).

20. *See* 34 C.F.R. § 104.39. "A recipient that operates a private elementary or secondary education program may not, on the basis of handicap, exclude a qualified handicapped person from such program if the person can, with minor adjustments, be provided with an appropriate education, as defined within [34 C.F.R. §] 104.33(b)(1), within the recipient's program."

21. *See Hunt v. St. Peter School*, 963 F. Supp. 843 (W.D. Mo. 1997) (rejecting a request that a school be made scent free on the basis that it was not a minor modification).

22. *Sullivan v. Vallejo City Unified School District*, 731 F. Supp. 947 (E.D. Cal 1990).

23. *Thomas v. Davidson Academy*, 662 F. Supp. 376 (M.D. Tenn. 1994).

24. *Jones v. Illinois Dep't of Rehab. Servs.*, 689 F.2d 724 (7th Cir. 1982).

25. *AP ex rel. Peterson v. Anoka-Hennepin Indep. School Dist. No. 11*, 538 F. Supp.2d 1125(D. Minn. 2008).

26. *Benedict v. Central Catholic High School*, 511 F. Supp.2d 854 (N.D. Ohio 2007).

27. *Hunt v. St. Peter School*, 963 F. Supp. 843 (W.D. Mo. 1997). *But see Barnes v. Converse College*, 436 F. Supp. (D.S.C. 1977) (ordering a college to provide an interpreter, at its own expense, for a hearing impaired teacher who was admitted to a summer program).

28. *Sherman v. Mamaroneck Union Free School Dist.*, 340 F.3d 87 (2d Cir. 2003).

29. At least one court has held that Section 504 does not require affirmative efforts to overcome a student's disability but only prohibits discrimination on the basis of the disability. *See Lyons v. Smith*, 829 F. Supp. 414 (D.D.C. 1993).

30. Another major difference between the laws is that the federal government provides public schools with direct federal financial assistance to help fund programs under the IDEA but does not offer any financial incentives to aid institutions, public and nonpublic, as they seek to comply with the dictates of Section 504.

31. *See, e.g., Guckenberger v. Boston University*, 8 F. Supp. 2d 82 (D. Mass. 1998) (upholding the decision of university officials not to permit students with learning disabilities to make course substitutions for its foreign language where other means of accommodating them were available).

32. *Southeastern Community College v. Davis*, 442 U.S. 397, 410 (1979) (upholding a nursing program's refusal to admit a student with a learning disability). *See also Alexander v. Choate*, 469 U.S. 287 (1985) (ruling that Section 504 only requires reasonable modification and not substantial changes), *Wynne v. Tufts Univ. School of Med.*, 976 F.2d 791 (1st Cir. 1992), *cert. denied* 507 U.S. 1030 (1993) (holding that medical school did not have to offer an alternative form of an examination to a student with a learning disability since this would have been a substantial alteration in the program and would have lowered standards).

33. *Davis, id.* at 412. *See also William S. v. Gill*, 572 F. Supp. 509 (E.D. Ill. 1983) (deciding that Section 504 did not require a school board to send a student to a private residential facility if the cost of doing so far exceeded that of having him remain in a public school).

34. *See School Bd. of Nassau County v. Arline*, 480 U.S. 273, 287-88 (1987) (setting forth the criteria for determining whether, under Section 504, a teacher with tuberculosis posed a significant health risk to the school community). *See also Doe v. Woodford County*, 213 F.3d 921 (6th Cir. 2000) (affirming that school officials in Kentucky could keep a student off of a junior varsity basketball team while they assessed whether his being a carrier of the hepatitis B virus presented a direct threat to the health and safety of others).

35. *See Cave v. East Meadow Union Free School Dist.*, 514 F.3d 240 (2d Cir. 2008) (although this case was dismissed on procedural grounds because the plaintiffs had failed to exhaust their administrative remedies, the trial court noted the concerns of school officials that the service dog could pose a potential threat to staff and students who had allergies).

36. 34 C.F.R. § 104.4(b)(3).

37. 34 C.F.R. § 104.34(c).

38. 34 C.F.R. § 104.39(b).

39. 34 C.F.R. § 104.36.

40. 34 C.F.R. § 104.5.

41. 34 C.F.R. § 104.35 Evaluation and placement.

> (a) Preplacement evaluation. A recipient that operates a public elementary or secondary education program or activity shall conduct an evaluation in accordance with the requirements of paragraph (b) of this section of any person who, because of handicap, needs or is believed to need special education or related services before taking any action with respect

to the initial placement of the person in regular or special education and any subsequent significant change in placement.

(b) Evaluation procedures. A recipient to which this subpart applies shall establish standards and procedures for the evaluation and placement of persons who, because of handicap, need or are believed to need special education or related services which ensure that:

(1) Tests and other evaluation materials have been validated for the specific purpose for which they are used and are administered by trained personnel in conformance with the instructions provided by their producer;

(2) Tests and other evaluation materials include those tailored to assess specific areas of educational need and not merely those which are designed to provide a single general intelligence quotient; and

(3) Tests are selected and administered so as best to ensure that, when a test is administered to a student with impaired sensory, manual, or speaking skills, the test results accurately reflect the student's aptitude or achievement level or whatever other factor the test purports to measure, rather than reflecting the student's impaired sensory, manual, or speaking skills (except where those skills are the factors that the test purports to measure).

(c) Placement procedures. In interpreting evaluation data and in making placement decisions, a recipient shall (1) draw upon information from a variety of sources, including aptitude and achievement tests, teacher recommendations, physical condition, social or cultural background, and adaptive behavior, (2) establish procedures to ensure that information obtained from all such sources is documented and carefully considered, (3) ensure that the placement decision is made by a group of persons, including persons knowledgeable about the child, the meaning of the evaluation data, and the placement options, and (4) ensure that the placement decision is made in conformity with § 104.34.

(d) Reevaluation. A recipient to which this section applies shall establish procedures, in accordance with paragraph (b) of this section, for periodic reevaluation of students who have been provided special education and related services. A reevaluation procedure consistent with the Education for the Handicapped Act is one means of meeting this requirement.

42. *See St. Johnsbury Academy v. D.H.*, 240 F.3d 163 (2d Cir. 2001).

43. *See, e.g., Tips v. Regents of Texas Tech University*, 921 F. Supp. 1515 (N.D. Tex. 1996) (rejecting the claim that the inability to organize material conceptually on a doctoral comprehensive examination was a disability within the meaning of Section 504).

44. *See, e.g., Argen v. New York State Board of Law Examiners*, 860 F. Supp. 84 (W.D.N.Y. 1994) (where an applicant failed to prove by a preponderance of the evidence that he was learning disabled).

45. *See, e.g., Price v. National Board of Medical Examiners*, 966 F. Supp. 419 (S.D. W. Va. 1997) (finding that three students with attention deficit hyperactivity disorder failed to show any substantial limitation on learning ability that would require additional time and a separate room for taking an examination) and *Gonzalez v. National Board of Medical Examiners*, 60 F. Supp.2d 703 (E.D. Mich. 1999) (upholding the board's refusal to grant extra time for examinations for a student whose scores on several other examinations were in the average to superior range).

46. *See, e.g., Begay v. Hodel*, 730 F. Supp. 1001 (D. Ariz. 1990).

47. *Sullivan v. Vallejo City Unified School District*, 731 F. Supp. 947 (E.D. Cal. 1990); *but see Cave v. East Meadow Union Free School Dist.*, 514 F.3d 240 (2d Cir. 2008).

48. *Eva N. v. Brock*, 741 F. Supp. 626 (E.D. Ky. 1990); *Kohl v. Woodhaven Learning Ctr.*, 865 F.2d 930 (8th Cir. 1989). *Also see Roberts v. Kindercare Learning Centers*, 896 F.2d 921 (D. Minn. 1995) (although decided under the ADA, the court ruled that requiring a day care center to provide a one-on-one personal care attendant for a developmentally delayed child would fundamentally alter the nature of its service).

4

INDIVIDUALS WITH DISABILITIES EDUCATION ACT

When the Individuals with Disabilities Education Act (IDEA) originally became law in 1975, it was known as the Education for All Handicapped Children Act.[1] The IDEA was revised in 1986, underwent a name change in 1990, and was reauthorized again in 1997 and 2004; the 2004 version of the IDEA became fully effective on July 1, 2005.[2]

Unlike Section 504, which has fairly broad standards, in order to qualify for services under the IDEA, students with disabilities must meet three statutory requirements. First, children must be between the ages of three and twenty-one.[3] Second, children must have specifically identified disabilities.[4] Third, children must be in need of special education[5] and related services,[6] meaning that they must be in need of a free appropriate public education (FAPE)[7] in the least restrictive environment that conforms to an individualized education program (IEP).[8] The IDEA defines an IEP as "a written statement for each child with a disability that is developed, reviewed, and revised in accordance with section 1414(d) of this title."[9]

In light of the IDEA's far-reaching impact, this chapter provides a general overview of the statute. Even though readers of this book are more likely to be interested in what the IDEA means for non-public schools, any understanding of the law would be incomplete without examining its broad terms with an eye as to how they influence public education.

INDIVIDUALIZED EDUCATION PROGRAMS

IEPs, which are essentially contractual agreements between parents, on behalf of their children, and school boards, must contain statements of students' current educational performance, annual goals and short-term objectives, the specific educational services to be provided, the extent to which the child can participate in general education, the date of initiation and duration of services, and evaluation criteria to assess whether the objectives are being met. IEPs must also include statements concerning how a child's disability affects his or her ability to be involved in and progress in the general educational curriculum along with statements regarding any modifications that may be needed to allow the child to participate in the general curriculum.[10] Children with disabilities are also entitled to related services[11] to assist them in benefitting from their special education programming.

The IDEA includes extensive due process protections safeguarding the rights of children[12] and their parents.[13] Among these protections, parents must be informed before consenting to initial evaluations[14] which must occur within sixty days of when educational officials received consent to conduct them,[15] and/or placements of their children[16] and have the right to take part in developing IEPs that direct the education of their children.[17]

IEPs must be developed by teams that are identified by various names such as child study team, multidisciplinary teams, and committees on special education depending on state law and local custom. IEPs must describe students' current levels of educational performance, annual goals and short-term objectives, the specific services that they will receive, the extent to which they can take part in general education, the date services are to begin and how long they will be offered, and criteria to evaluate whether they are achieving their goals.[18] Moreover, IEPs must discuss how students' disabilities affect their ability to be involved in and progress in inclusive settings and necessary modifications to allow them to take part in the general curriculum. IEPs must also detail related services that students need to benefit from their IEPs.[19] A new provision in the 2004 version of the IDEA specifies that IEP teams are no longer required to develop benchmarks and short-term objectives for children with disabilities other than for those who take alternate assessments aligned to alternate achievement standards.[20]

When assessments are completed, and children are identified as being in need of IEPs, school officials must convene IEP meetings within thirty calendar days.[21] When IEPs are developed, officials must implement them "[a]s soon as possible."[22]

IEP teams must include a child's parents who have the right to participate actively in their development; at least one of a student's regular education teachers if the child is, or will be participating, in regular education; at least one special education teacher or, if appropriate, one of the child's special education providers; a representative of the school board who is qualified to provide, or supervise, the delivery of special education, knowledgeable about general education, the board's resources, and evaluation procedures; an individual who can interpret the instructional implications of evaluation results; others, at the discretion of parents or boards, who are knowledgeable or have special expertise concerning the student; and, when appropriate, the child.[23] If students attend non-public schools, a representative of those schools should be present at IEP conferences.[24]

In addition to its IEP provisions, the IDEA includes an elaborate system of procedural safeguards to protect the rights of children and their parents.[25] However, as discussed below, other than for its child find provisions, the IDEA's procedural safeguards are generally inapplicable to complaints that school boards failed to deliver services to students in non-public schools.[26] The IDEA also includes provisions, supplemented by the Family Education Rights and Privacy Act (FERPA),[27] FERPA's accompanying regulations,[28] and the IDEA's own regulations,[29] preserving the confidentiality of all information used in the evaluation, placement, and education of students.

When dealing with non-public schools, regardless of whether they are religiously affiliated, it is important to note that according to a federal regulation, FERPA "does not apply to an educational agency or institution solely because students attending that agency or institution receive nonmonetary benefits under a program referenced in paragraph (a) of this section, if no funds under that program are made available to the agency or institution."[30] Even though this standard excludes non-public schools from the reach of FERPA, officials in these schools would be wise to develop policies safeguarding student records.

Once students have been placed in special education, school board officials must provide parents with proper notice before initiating a change in placement.[31] Once placed, a child's situation must be reviewed at least annually[32] and the student must be reevaluated completely at least every three years, unless the parents and school officials agree that a complete reevaluation is unnecessary.[33]

In a provision that can create some difficulties, especially when parents are paying tuition in non-public schools, when children with disabilities who are not adjudicated incompetent under state law achieve the age of majority, school officials must notify them and their parents that the parental rights of access have been transferred to their children.[34] The IDEA includes a special rule for students with disabilities who are not adjudicated incompetent but lack the ability to provide informed consent with respect to their educational programming. In such situations, officials must establish procedures for appointing their parents, or if they are not available, other appropriate persons, to represent students' educational interests throughout their remaining period of eligibility under the IDEA.[35]

Teams must review IEPs at least annually[36] and reevaluate them at least once every three years unless parents and local school officials agree that reevaluations are unnecessary.[37] The 2004 IDEA includes three noteworthy changes with regard to IEPs. First, the IDEA no longer specifies the need for benchmarks and short-term objectives for children with disabilities other than those who take alternate assessments aligned to alternate achievement standards.[38] Second, up to fifteen states are free to pilot comprehensive multiyear IEPs that do not exceed three years and which are designed to coincide with natural transition points in a child's education.[39] Third, minor changes to IEPs can be made via conference calls or letters.[40] As children near high school graduation or begin to "age out" of special education, educators must develop individualized transition services plans to promote their movement to post-school activities.[41]

Under the IDEA, when children are placed in special education settings, school officials must notify parents before trying to change their placements.[42] Parents may be entitled to independent evaluations at public expense if they disagree with school board evaluations[43] or are unhappy with proposed placements. Parents who successfully challenge the assessments of their children can be reimbursed for the costs of doing so. If hearing officers or courts reject parental challenges in determining that board evaluations were appropriate, they are not entitled to further testing at public expense.[44] At the same time, a board may challenge a parental request for an independent evaluation in an administrative hearing, and if it turns out that the board's evaluation was appropriate, the parents are not entitled to have an independent evaluation at public expense.[45]

APPROPRIATE PLACEMENT

The IDEA requires school boards to provide a continuum of alternative FAPEs for all students with disabilities[46] at no expense to their parents. Moreover, if parents have insurance, they can be asked to file claims to help defray costs associated with the education of their children with special needs.[47] Even so, school officials cannot refuse to provide services if parents are unwilling, or unable, to place claims with their insurance companies.

As important as the "appropriate" component of FAPE is, the IDEA offers little guidance in defining what may be considered appropriate beyond indicating that an appropriate education consists of special education and related services that are provided in conformance with an IEP.[48] Insofar as a precise definition of the term *appropriate* cannot be found in either the statute or its regulations, it is necessary to turn to judicial interpretation for further guidance on the meaning of FAPE.

In *Board of Education of the Hendrick Hudson Central School District v. Rowley* (*Rowley*),[49] the Supreme Court offered a minimal definition of a FAPE. *Rowley* arose when the parents of a kindergarten student in New York who was hearing impaired protested their school board's refusal to provide their daughter with a sign-language interpreter.[50] Lower federal courts ordered the school board to provide the interpreter on the basis that an appropriate education was one that would have allowed the child to achieve at a level commensurate with that of her peers who were not disabled.

The Supreme Court, noting that the child in *Rowley* was achieving passing marks and advancing from grade to grade without the sign-language interpreter, reversed in favor of the school board. The Court held that an appropriate education was one that was formulated in accordance with all of the IDEA's procedures and is "sufficient to confer some educational benefit"[51] on a child with a disability. Insofar as the child in *Rowley* received some educational benefit without the sign-language interpreter, the Court was convinced that educators were not required to provide one even though she might have achieved at a higher level with the services.

Rowley establishes a minimum standard of what constitutes a FAPE under federal law. At the same time, courts have upheld higher state requirements in California,[52] Michigan,[53] Missouri,[54] New Jersey,[55] and North Carolina.[56] Conversely, under West Virginia law, "no state rule, policy or standard under this article or any county board rule, policy or standard governing special education may exceed the requirements of federal law or regulation."[57] In some of these cases, courts have explicitly acknowledged that the higher state standards replaced the federal requirements.

The *Rowley* standard has been further refined[58] as courts have indicated that the "some educational benefit" criteria requires more than just minimal or trivial benefits.[59] Other courts have expanded the criteria by deciding that an educational benefit must be meaningful[60] or appreciable.[61] One court went so far as to maintain that a student's gains must be measurable to meet the *Rowley* criteria.[62] Regardless of which criteria are employed, subsequent case law has made it clear that under the IDEA's so-called zero-reject approach, each child with a disability must be served.[63]

LEAST RESTRICTIVE ENVIRONMENT

According to the IDEA, all students with disabilities must be educated in the least restrictive environment (LRE).[64] In two cases, federal appellate courts directed school boards to place students with disabilities in regular education settings as opposed to segregated special education classrooms. The courts agreed that educators must consider a variety of factors when formulating a child's LRE.

In *Oberti v. Board of Education of the Borough of Clementon School District*,[65] a case from New Jersey, the Third Circuit adopted a two-part test for assessing compliance with the LRE requirement. The first element of the test is whether education in the regular classroom, with the use of supplementary aids and services, can be achieved satisfactorily. The second part of the test adds that if a placement outside of the regular classroom is necessary, educators must consider whether a child was mainstreamed (now referred to as full inclusion) to the maximum extent appropriate.[66]

As described by the Ninth Circuit in *Sacramento City Unified School District Board of Education v. Rachel H.*,[67] a dispute from California, four factors must be addressed in making a placement: the educational benefits of placing a child with a disability in a regular classroom; the nonacademic benefits of such a placement; the effect that the student's presence would have on the teacher and other children in the class; and the costs of an inclusionary placement. Educators must take all of these into account in placing a student with a disability.

Inherent in both of these cases is the principle that educators must make reasonable efforts to place students with disabilities in fully inclusive settings by providing them with supplementary aids and services to ensure success. Even with the focus on inclusion, not all students with disabilities must be placed in regular education classes. Courts have approved segregated settings where educators demonstrated that students with disabilities could not function in regular classrooms or would not benefit in such settings, even with supplementary aids and services.[68] The bottom line is that an inclusionary placement should be the setting of choice and a segregated setting should be contemplated only if an inclusionary placement has failed despite the best efforts of educators or there is overwhelming evidence that it is not feasible.

PRIVATE AND RESIDENTIAL SCHOOL PLACEMENTS

The IDEA's preference for full inclusion is not feasible for all students. Even so, the IDEA does require school officials to offer a continuum of placement alternatives to meet the educational needs of children with disabilities.[69] In this regard, public school officials may be required to place children in non-public schools when boards lack appropriate placements,[70] such as when a student has a low incidence disability and there are not enough children with the same type of disability within the system to warrant the development of a program.[71] These courts have recognized that since smaller school boards probably cannot afford to develop specialized programs for small numbers of students, they must look elsewhere for placements.

Courts may order residential placements for students with severe, profound, or multiple disabilities[72] if they require twenty-four-hour-per-day programming or consistency between their school and home environments. Residential placements may also be necessary for students with significant behavioral disorders[73] or who require total immersion in educational environments in order to progress.[74]

If residential placements are required for purely educational reasons, school boards must pay the full cost and cannot require parents to contribute toward their cost.[75] If placements are made for other than educational reasons such as for medical or social purposes, then school systems may only be required to pay for the educational component of the residential settings[76] but may also enter into a cost-share agreement with other agencies.

In the first of two cases that are illustrative of these issues, the Seventh Circuit affirmed that a mother in Illinois who, due to her failure to cooperate by refusing to give school officials a reasonable opportunity to evaluate her son, forfeited any claim to tuition reimbursement for unilaterally placing him in a private school.[77] The court rejected the mother's request because after her son was not permitted to return to a religiously affiliated school she enrolled him in a private residential facility without first affording public school personnel the opportunity to evaluate his condition. Conversely, a federal trial court in Indiana awarded partial reimbursement where the non-public school chosen by the parents provided their son with an appropriate education but they failed to notify the school board in writing of their intent to enroll him there at public expense.[78] The court also commented that the board failed to provide the student with an appropriate program.

EXTENDED SCHOOL YEAR PROGRAMS

If students with disabilities require educational programs that extend beyond the time when regular school years operate, boards must provide such placements at public expense.[79] Extended school year programs are generally necessary when students regress and the time it takes to recoup lost skills interferes with overall progress toward the attainment of the goals and objectives in their IEPs.[80] Regression that students experience must be greater than that which ordinarily occurs during school vacations. If regressions are minimal, boards are not obligated to provide extended school year programs.[81]

CHILD FIND

The IDEA regulations require states, through local educational agencies or school boards, to identify, locate, and evaluate all children with disabilities,[82] including those who attend religiously affiliated non-public schools,[83] regardless of the severity of their disabilities.

Insofar as the duty of locating, identifying, and serving students in need of special education is generally delegated to individual school boards, officials typically disseminate information about the services available to students with disabilities via newspaper articles, radio announcements, and advertisements on cable television. In addition, many school officials may leave information pamphlets in locations frequented by parents of young children, such as pediatricians' offices, day care centers, private preschools, places of worship, and shopping malls.

To the extent that the IDEA categorizes the early identification and assessment of children with disabilities as a related service,[84] it is common for school boards to offer annual screenings for preschool- and kindergarten-aged children. While the kindergarten screening process is generally conducted as part of the normal kindergarten registration activities, educators usually set up special dates to screen preschool-aged children. Further, a parent who suspects that his or her child has a disability can ask for a screening by appointment at any time during a school year.

As discussed below, the IDEA made significant changes in 2004 relating to the "child find" activities undertaken to locate students in non-public schools who have disabilities. In a recent change, officials in public school must identify children with disabilities whose parents enrolled them in non-public schools in the districts where they attend class rather than where they live.[85] These officials must provide accurate counts to state education agencies on the number of children from non-public schools whom they have evaluated, identified as having disabilities, and served.[86] In addition, officials must use child find activities for students in non-public schools that are similar to those used to identify children who attend public schools.[87]

MINIMUM COMPETENCY TESTS

As many states have moved toward adopting high-stakes testing in the call for greater accountability in the nation's classrooms, it is important to focus on legal issues surrounding minimum competency tests (MCTs). MCTs may be used either as a graduation requirement to assure that students receiving a diploma have a specified knowledge base or to identify students who have not achieved competency in basic skills and may require remedial instruction. Insofar as the IDEA requires students with disabilities to participate in some form of state assessments,[88] the accountability provisions of the No Child Left Behind Act, which requires local school systems to make adequate yearly progress,[89] may ultimately have a major impact on the delivery of special education services.

States clearly have the authority to develop and administer MCTs and to establish graduation requirements. It is well settled that states may require students to pass MCTs to receive standard high school diplomas as long as they satisfy three primary guidelines. First, when these tests are used as a graduation requirement, they must not only be a valid, reliable measure of what has been taught but must also afford students sufficient notice that they must pass MCTs to receive standard diplomas.[90] Second, consistent with the nondiscrimination standards in the IDEA's evaluation procedures,[91] MCTs may not be racially, linguistically, or ethnically discriminatory.[92] Third, in order to have students with disabilities take, and pass, an MCT before receiving a standard high school diploma,[93] along with sufficient notice of an examination, their IEPs should specifically identify areas in need of instruction so that they can be prepared for the test.

Similar to the accommodations that may be required for admissions testing under Section 504, students with disabilities taking MCTs may be entitled to modifications. School officials may be required to modify how a test is administered but are not obligated to change an examination's actual content or offer an alternate test. For example, a student who is blind should be given a braille version of the test while a child with a physical disability should be offered any necessary assistance writing or filling in the circles on a machine-scored answer sheet. It is unlikely that a school board will be required to develop and administer a test with fewer items or easier items for a student with intellectual impairments.[94]

Basically, school officials are obligated to provide modifications that will allow a student to take a test but do not need to modify the item content or compromise its validity. In such a situation, the Office of Civil Rights (OCR) entered an order in favor of a school board in Florida where educational officials rejected a parent's request that a proctor be permitted to read an MCT to her child. In observing that since the communications section of the examination was designed to test the student's reading and comprehension skills, OCR was of the view that school officials had the authority to reject the mother's request since granting it would have compromised the validity of the test.[95]

As part of teams, parents of children with disabilities are responsible for working with other members of an IEP team in determining the components of their child's IEP.[96] School officials should make parents aware of the general content of tests, where and how they are to be administered, and the purposes for which the results are to be used. Following an evaluation period, and prior to placement, a decision should be made regarding the appropriateness of including MCT material in a child's IEP. If an IEP team is satisfied that such content is inappropriate, the parents may always appeal to an impartial hearing officer. Consequently, to the extent that educators routinely follow these practices, and keep parents involved, they are unlikely to face the threat of litigation involving proficiency testing of students with disabilities.

RELATED SERVICES

School boards must provide related, or supportive, services to each child with a disability if they are necessary to help the student to benefit from special education. The IDEA specifically lists developmental, supportive, or corrective services such as transportation, speech pathology, audiology, psychological services, physical therapy, occupational therapy, recreation (including therapeutic recreation), social work services, counseling services (including rehabilitation counseling), medical services (for diagnostic or evaluative purposes only), and early identification and assessment as related services.[97] The only limit on what can be a related service is that medical services are exempted unless they are specifically for diagnostic or evaluative purposes.

One of the most controversial topics under the rubric of related services involves the distinction between medical and school health services. Procedures that must, by law, be performed by a licensed physician would be exempted medical services. Thus, psychiatric therapy would not be a related service since a psychiatrist is a licensed physician. Further, an addition to the IDEA makes it clear that related services do not include medical devices that are surgically implanted or the replacement of such devices.[98]

Many students with significant medical needs require round-the-clock nursing services, a service that falls somewhere on the continuum between school health services and medical services. The Supreme Court first addressed this issue in *Irving Independent School District v. Tatro*,[99] when it held that a service such as catheterization that can be performed by a school nurse or trained layperson is a required related service under the IDEA. More recently, the Court extended its rationale in *Cedar Rapids Community School District v. Garret F.*,[100] in finding that regardless of cost, a school board was required to provide, and pay for, a full-time nurse while a student was in school since his medical condition required constant nursing services.[101]

ASSISTIVE TECHNOLOGY

A potentially costly service involves assistive technology. The 1990 IDEA amendments added definitions of assistive technology devices and services. The 1997 and 2004 versions of the IDEA clarified and expanded these definitions. The IDEA and its regulations define assistive technology devices as items, pieces of equipment, or product systems that are used to increase, maintain, or improve the functional capabilities of students with disabilities. These devices may include commercially available, modified, or customized equipment.[102] This definition excludes surgically implanted medical devices.[103]

The IDEA and its regulations define assistive technology services as services that are designed to directly assist an individual with a disability in the selection, acquisition, or use of an assistive technology device.[104] Assistive technology services includes an evaluation of a student's needs, including a functional evaluation of the individual in the child's customary environment; considering whether to purchase, lease, or otherwise provide for the acquisition of the assistive technology device; selecting, designing, fitting, customizing, adapting, applying, maintaining, repairing, or replacing the assistive technology device; coordinating and using other therapies, interventions, or services with assistive technology devices such as those associated with existing education and rehabilitation programs; training or providing technical assistance for the student or his or her family; and making training and technical assistance available to professionals who provide education or rehabilitation services as well as to employers or other individuals who offer services to the student with disabilities.

As extensive as its reach is, it is surprising that assistive technology is not specifically included in either the definition of special education or related services. Assistive technology does fit within the definition of special education as specially designed instruction and within the definition of related services as a developmental, corrective, or supportive service. Yet, instead of including assistive technology within either of these two definitions, Congress chose to create assistive technology as a category separate from special education and related services. Accordingly, assistive technology can be considered special education services, related services, or supplementary aids or services. Regardless of which rubric they may be covered by, school boards are required to provide students with disabilities with supplementary aids and services to allow them to be educated in the least restrictive environment.[105]

As indicated above, assistive technology may be provided as a special education service, a related service, or as a supplementary aid and/or service. Assistive technology is required when it is necessary for a student to receive a FAPE under the *Rowley* standard. Further, assistive technology may allow many students with disabilities to benefit from education in less restrictive settings and so may also be required under the IDEA's least restrictive environment provision. IEP teams are required to consider whether students require assistive technology devices and services in order to receive an appropriate education.[106] Even so, no provisions direct IEP teams to document their discussions of students' assistive technology needs and whether they were required. If teams determine that assistive technology is required, this must be written into students' IEPs.

School board officials are required to ensure that assistive technology devices and services are made available to a child if either or both are required as part of the student's special education, related services, or supplementary aids and services.[107] Additionally, the use of school-provided assistive technology devices is required in a student's home if an IEP team decides that the child needs access to assistive technology in order to receive a FAPE.[108]

In explanatory material accompanying the 1999 regulations, the Department of Education made it clear that school boards are not required to provide personal devices, such as eyeglasses, hearing aids, and/or braces, that a student would require regardless of whether the child attended school.[109] Students with disabilities are entitled to access any general technology that is available to peers who are not disabled. If students with disabilities need accommodations in order to use general technology, they must be provided.[110]

REMEDIES

If school board officials fail to provide students with disabilities with a FAPE, parents have a variety of remedies available, starting with mediation and due process hearings. Once parents have completed the administrative process, they can seek judicial relief. To this end, the IDEA authorizes the courts to grant appropriate relief based on the records of administrative proceedings, hear additional evidence at the request of a party, and grant relief based on the preponderance of the evidence standard.[111] Frequently, the courts order school officials to provide specified special education and related services. However, as discussed below in the section on tuition reimbursement, if parents unilaterally obtain the necessary services at their own expense, a court may direct a school board to reimburse them for all legitimate expenses.

PROCEDURAL DUE PROCESS

Subject to the discussion below in the section on complaints, the IDEA's extensive due process procedures do not apply to students who attend non-public schools. In public school settings, if parents disagree with any of a school board's actions regarding a proposed IEP or any aspect of a FAPE, they may seek mediation.[112] However, since mediation is voluntary, it may not be used to deny or delay parental requests for administrative hearings. A new provision of the IDEA that was incorporated with the 2004 amendments requires school officials to conduct meetings with parents for the purpose of attempting to resolve disputes before due process hearings are convened.[113] These meetings must be scheduled within fifteen days of the parents' request for a hearing and a representative of the school board who has decision-making authority must be in attendance. Both parties may waive the resolution session, or alternatively, may use the mediation process.[114]

Parents who are dissatisfied can also invoke their right to due process hearings[115] which must be presided over by fair and impartial third-party decision makers.[116] Insofar as parents whose children attend non-public schools are ordinarily not entitled to this form of relief, suffice it to say that hearings involve the calling of witnesses and decisions based on the records of the proceedings. Parties that are dissatisfied with the final result of administrative proceedings may appeal to the state or federal courts;[117] before doing so, an aggrieved party must exhaust all administrative remedies unless it is futile to do so. While administrative or judicial actions are pending, pursuant to the IDEA's so-called stay-put provisions, children must remain in their then current placements, meaning that school officials may not change students' placements unless they obtain parental consent,[118] orders from hearing officers,[119] or judicial decrees.[120]

As noted, the IDEA empowers the courts to review the record of the administrative proceedings, hear additional evidence, and "grant such relief as the court determines is appropriate" based on the preponderance of evidence standard.[121] At the same time, the Supreme Court has cautioned judges not to substitute their views of proper educational methodology for that of competent school authorities.[122] In a significant addition, the 2004 version of the IDEA includes a two-year limitations period during which parties can request due process hearings.[123] If state laws set different limitations periods, then those periods prevail. The IDEA adds that its statute of limitations is to be stayed if parents can show that school officials misrepresented that they resolved a disagreement or if they withheld pertinent information from the parents.[124]

The IDEA is not the exclusive avenue through which parents may enforce the rights of their child with disabilities. The IDEA specifically stipulates that none of its provisions can be interpreted as restricting or limiting the rights, procedures, and remedies available under the Constitution, Section 504, or other federal statutes protecting the rights of students with disabilities.[125] Litigation is often initiated under Section 504, the ADA, and Section 1983 of the Civil Rights Act of 1871[126] in addition to the IDEA.

DAMAGES

Courts generally have not imposed punitive damages on school authorities for failing to provide a FAPE to a child with a disability.[127] Similarly, general damages awards for "pain and suffering" have not been prevalent.[128] Recent litigation indicates that this may be changing.[129] Courts have remarked that monetary damages may be available under other statutes, such as Section 504, if parents can show that school officials intentionally discriminated against their child or egregiously disregarded the student's rights.[130] The operative word here is intentionally. If school officials act in good faith but their efforts fall short of meeting statutory requirements, they should be immune from damages.

TUITION REIMBURSEMENT

Sometimes parents who are dissatisfied with placements unilaterally enroll their children in private schools and seek to recover tuition expenses. In *Burlington School Committee v. Department of Education, Commonwealth of Massachusetts*,[131] the Supreme Court ruled that parents are entitled to tuition reimbursement if they can show that school boards failed to offer a FAPE and that their chosen placements in private schools were appropriate. The Court reasoned that awarding reimbursement simply requires school boards to pay retroactively the costs that they should have been paying all along.

Eight years later, in *Florence County School District Four v. Carter* (*Carter*),[132] the Supreme Court found that parents are entitled to reimbursement even if their chosen placements are not in state-approved facilities as long as they provided children with educations that were otherwise appropriate. Even so, when parents unilaterally place their children, they do so at their own financial risk because they are not entitled to reimbursement if school officials can show that they offered, and could provide, an appropriate educational placement. Parents are also entitled to reimbursement for unilaterally obtained related services if they can demonstrate that a school board failed to provide the needed services.

Parents, frustrated with their children's educational programs, frequently remove them from the public schools and unilaterally enroll them in private schools that provide special education services. Often these schools offer low staff-to-student ratios so that the children receive more individualized attention than they did in the public schools.

Under *Carter* parents can be reimbursed for unilateral private school placements even when their chosen schools are not state-approved special education facilities. Courts are mixed as to whether parents can be reimbursed for tuition expenses when the schools do not provide the special education services the students require. For example, in a recent case, the Second Circuit reversed a lower court's tuition reimbursement award because the parents' chosen school did not offer the student the special education services he needed.[133] On the other hand, in a dispute from Pennsylvania, the Third Circuit affirmed an award of tuition reimbursement for a placement at a nonapproved facility where faculty and staff were not certified in special education after determining that the student made progress while he was enrolled there.[134]

Courts have even awarded reimbursements for tuition in religiously affiliated non-public schools where parents have shown that their public schools failed to provide appropriate educational placements and the religious schools met the students' needs.[135] In such a case, the federal trial court in Massachusetts specifically ruled that awarding tuition reimbursement for a parental placement in a religious school did not violate the First Amendment since the funds would go toward paying for the child's appropriate education under the IDEA without regard for his religious orientation.[136] Whether tuition can be awarded for religious schools may also depend on state law.[137]

COMPENSATORY SERVICES

Tuition reimbursement is likely to be of little use to parents who are unable to place their children unilaterally in non-public schools because they cannot afford to pay for tuition and related expenses. When parents cannot afford to make unilateral placements, their children may remain in inappropriate settings while disputes wind their way through due process hearings and judicial proceedings. In such situations, courts may award additional educational services and prospective relief to compensate the parents, and child, for the loss of appropriate educational services.

The courts have pointed out that compensatory services, like reimbursement, compensate students and their parents for the failure of school boards to provide children with a FAPE. The rationale behind awards of compensatory services is that appropriate remedies should not be available only to students whose parents can afford to provide them with alternate educational placements while litigation is pending.[138] Generally, compensatory services are provided for periods of time equal to that for which the children were denied services[139] and may be granted even after students have passed the ceiling age for eligibility under the IDEA.[140]

In a recent case dealing with compensatory services, the Eleventh Circuit affirmed that an eighteen-year-old student in Georgia who read at a third grade level due to his learning disabilities was entitled to compensatory services where school officials failed either to evaluate his progress for more than five years or to implement his IEP in a timely fashion.[141] In specifying that the trial court was placing the student in the position that he would have been in had school officials done their jobs properly, the Eleventh Circuit noted that he was entitled to a placement in a private school for about five years or until he graduated high school, whichever came first. As with tuition reimbursement, awards of compensatory educational services are granted only when hearing officers or courts have ascertained that school boards failed to provide students with appropriate placements.

ATTORNEY FEES AND OTHER EXPENSES

It almost goes without saying that litigation can cost a great deal. Many parents, after prevailing in court against a school board, reasonably expect to be reimbursed for their expenses in safeguarding the educational rights of their children. Parents argued that they achieved hollow victories when they prevailed but were left with burdensome legal bills.

In 1984 the Supreme Court held that recovery of legal expenses was not available under the IDEA.[142] Two years later Congress responded by amending the IDEA with the passage of the Handicapped Children's Protection Act (HCPA).[143] The HCPA gave courts the power to award reasonable attorney fees to parents who prevailed against school boards in actions or proceedings brought pursuant to the IDEA. An award must be based on the prevailing rates in the community in which the case arose.

Under the HCPA, courts are free to determine what is a reasonable amount of time spent preparing and arguing a case. Awards may be limited if school boards made settlement offers more than ten days before the proceedings began that were equal to or more favorable than the final relief obtained.[144] Further, courts may reduce awards if they find that parents unreasonably protracted disputes,[145] the hourly rates of attorneys were excessive,[146] or the time spent and legal services furnished were excessive in light of the issues.[147] The Act does not permit parents who are attorneys to recover fees for representing their own children.[148] The HCPA was made retroactive to July 4, 1984, the day before the Supreme Court declared that attorney fees were unavailable under the IDEA.

After Congress modified the IDEA to allow parents who prevail in disputes with their school boards to recover attorney fees, the question of whether they could obtain the cost of expert witnesses remained unanswered. In the face of parental arguments that just as attorneys helped them to obtain services that their children should have had in the first place, so, too, expert witnesses assisted them in the same way, the courts reached mixed results as some granted these requests while others refused to provide reimbursements.

The Supreme Court agreed to resolve the issue in a case from New York, *Arlington Central School District v. Murphy.*[149] The Court held that absent clear congressional intent to make such a remedy available by including it in the IDEA's provisions, prevailing parents could not recover costs associated with hiring expert witnesses or consultants who assisted them in their disputes with school boards. Subject to congressional modification of the IDEA, then, parents are left without recourse when they seek to recover costs associated with expert witnesses and consultants who helped them to prevail in judicial actions against their school boards in safeguarding the educational rights of their children.

DISCIPLINE

Perhaps the most controversial legal issue in special education concerns disciplinary sanctions and students with disabilities.[150] In fact, until its 1997 Amendments were adopted, the IDEA did not make a direct reference to discipline. Disciplining students with disabilities is highly sensitive since it pits the duty of administrators to maintain order, discipline, and a safe environment against the rights of each child to receive a FAPE in the LRE. Even though most will agree that the power of school officials to maintain discipline should not be frustrated, it must be understood that a student should not be denied the rights accorded by the IDEA if misconduct is a manifestation of a child's disability.

School officials may impose a disciplinary sanction on a student in special education as long as they follow procedures that do not deprive a child of his or her rights. To this end, educators may use normal disciplinary sanctions, including suspensions, with special education students by following usual procedures and providing customary due process.[151] Administrators face some restrictions when they intend to impose more drastic punishments such as an expulsion or wish to change a student's placement for disciplinary reasons. Basically, in these situations, the due process procedures in the IDEA replace the normal due process protections.

Case law makes it clear that although a student with a disability cannot be expelled for misconduct that is a manifestation of his or her disability, a child can be excluded if there is no relationship between the misconduct and disability.[152] While the Supreme Court's landmark decision in *Honig v. Doe*[153] supported the prohibition against expelling students for disability-related misconduct, it did permit them to be suspended for up to ten days. During the ten-day cooling off period, school personnel may attempt to negotiate an alternative placement with a student's parents. If school officials are unsuccessful in negotiating an alternative placement with parents, and can show that a student is truly dangerous, they may obtain an injunction or order allowing them to exclude the child from school.

The 1997 Amendments, which codified case law since *Honig*, while clarifying many of the gaps in the statute, implemented the most far-reaching changes to the IDEA since it was enacted. The IDEA now contains specific requirements and provisions for disciplining students with disabilities.[154] The regulations explicitly state that the unilateral removal of a student with a disability from the child's current educational placement for more than ten consecutive school days constitutes an impermissible change of placement.[155]

In a major change, in 1997 the IDEA increased the authority of educators to deal with students with disabilities who possess weapons or drugs.[156] Under these provisions, educators may transfer a student with a disability to an interim alternative placement for up to forty-five days for possession of a weapon or possession, use, sale, or solicitation of drugs on school property or at a school function.[157] School officials may also order a change in placement to an interim alternative setting if this sanction is used for students who are not disabled under similar circumstances.[158] The IDEA, relying on another federal statute, now defines dangerous weapons as including instruments, devices, materials, and substances capable of inflicting harm in addition to firearms, but does not include small pocketknives.[159] The IDEA defines an illegal drug as a controlled substance, but excludes controlled substances that may be legally prescribed by physicians.[160]

The 2004 version of the IDEA added that educators can now remove students with disabilities to alternative educational placements for inflicting serious bodily injuries.[161] Again relying on another part of federal law,[162] the IDEA defines serious bodily injuries as involving a substantial risk of death, extreme physical pain, protracted and obvious disfigurement, or protracted loss or impairment of the function of a bodily member, organ, or mental faculty.[163] Serious bodily injury may be contrasted with bodily injury, which generally involves only cuts, abrasions, bruises, burns, or other temporary injuries.[164]

Once officials have moved students with disabilities to alternative placements for in excess of ten school days,[165] they must conduct functional behavioral assessments (FBAs) and implement behavioral intervention plans (BIPs) for children if they are not already in place.[166] If BIPs were in place when children misbehaved, IEP teams must review them and their implementation in order to make any necessary modifications.[167] More specifically, educators must perform FBAs and implement BIPs whenever students with disabilities are removed from their then current placements for disciplinary reasons for more than ten school days.[168] FBAs and BIPs must also be executed, if they have not already been done, if officials decide that student misbehaviors are not manifestations of their disabilities.[169]

Should a parent disagree with the alternative placement and request a hearing, consistent with the IDEA's stay-put provision, students must remain in their alternative settings.[170] When the forty-five-day periods expire, officials must return students to their former settings even if hearings on school board proposals to change their placements are pending unless parents and educators agree otherwise.[171]

The IDEA establishes procedures required to evaluate whether misconduct is related to a student's disability.[172] The IDEA calls for this judgment to be made by the team that developed the student's IEP[173] within ten school days of when it chose to take disciplinary action.[174] According to the IDEA, a manifestation is conduct that was caused by or had a direct and substantial relationship to students' disabilities or was the direct result of the failure of school officials to implement IEPs properly.[175] In reviewing whether placements were inappropriate, IEP teams should use the same standards that applied when they prospectively evaluated whether proposed placements were appropriate. In the event that IEP teams interpret misconduct as either a manifestation of students' disabilities or as a result of improperly implemented IEPs, children may not be expelled or suspended for more than ten days and school officials must reconsider their current placements.[176] In making manifestation determinations, IEP teams must consider all relevant information, including evaluations and diagnostic results as well as student observations.[177]

However, if IEP teams are convinced that acts of misbehavior by students are not manifestations of their disabilities, then children may be disciplined in the same manner as any students who are not disabled.[178] The disciplinary options available to educators do not forbid expulsion if it is the usual sanction for a particular misbehavior in question. Parents may challenge the results of manifestation determinations by requesting expedited due process hearings.[179] If parents do make such challenges, then educators must postpone long-term suspensions or expulsions until hearings have been completed, even though students may remain in their interim alternative educational settings.[180]

In 1997, the IDEA clarified whether school officials can discontinue educational services for students who are properly expelled for misconduct that is not disability related. This provision codified existing policy from the United States Department of Education which ordered the delivery of educational services in this situation and effectively reversed a controversial decision from Virginia wherein the Fourth Circuit held that no such requirement existed under the IDEA.[181] The IDEA made it clear that a FAPE must to be made available to all students with disabilities including those who have been expelled from school.[182] In other words, even if students with disabilities have been expelled in accord with the IDEA's provisions, children must be provided with services that will allow them to progress in general education curricula and achieve the goals of their IEPs.

It is important to keep in mind that students with disabilities can still be suspended for up to ten school days as long as the same penalties can be imposed on children who are not disabled.[183] Even so, as noted under such a circumstance, school officials must conduct FBAs, if they have not already done so, to address the students' infractions. The regulations do not require officials to provide services to a child who has been suspended for ten days or less. Nothing forbids educational officials from providing services to students who are excluded from school for less than ten days.

In a related concern, school officials must now provide the IDEA's protections to students if they knew, or should have known, that children had disabilities before the misbehavior occurred.[184] School officials are considered to have this knowledge if parents express concern that their children may need special education or make requests for evaluations. Educators may also be considered to be on notice of students' disabilities based on their prior behavioral and academic history and/or concerns expressed by their teachers.[185]

An exception to the IDEA's notice requirement exists if educators already conducted evaluations and decided that students did not have disabilities.[186] In addition, if parents refused permission for evaluations or declined offered special education services, school officials are not deemed to have knowledge of student disabilities.[187] If school board officials lack prior knowledge that students have disabilities, children may be disciplined in the same manner as peers who are not disabled.[188]

If parents make requests for evaluations when disciplinary sanctions have been imposed, they must be conducted in an expedited manner.[189] However, unlike guidelines for conducting expedited hearings, neither the IDEA nor its regulations establish time frames during which these evaluations must take place. Until these evaluations are completed, students must remain in the educational placements selected by school officials, meaning that they can be denied services while they are suspended or expelled.[190] If, following the evaluations, school officials are convinced that students do have disabilities, then they are entitled to special education and related services.[191]

A final element in the IDEA's discipline provisions explains that the law cannot be interpreted as prohibiting school officials from reporting crimes committed by students with disabilities to the proper authorities or impeding law enforcement and judicial authorities from carrying out their responsibilities.[192] When school officials do report crimes, they must furnish copies of students' special education and disciplinary records to the appropriate authorities[193] to the extent that they are permitted to do so under the FERPA.[194]

NOTES

1. The IDEA is still sometimes referred to as P.L. 94–142, noting that it was the 142nd piece of legislation introduced during the 94th Congress. For the sake of con-

sistency, this chapter refers to the law as the IDEA, which incorporated the changes in the Individuals with Disabilities Education Improvement Act, even for cases that were resolved before its 1990 reauthorization and name change. This book also refers to the most recent reauthorization of the IDEA as the 2004 version of the law.

2. For more complete discussions of the IDEA, *see* Charles J. Russo and Allan G. Osborne Jr., *Essential Concepts and School-Based Cases in Special Education Law* (Thousand Oaks, CA: Corwin Press, 2008); Allan G. Osborne Jr. and Charles J. Russo, *Special Education and the Law: A Guide for Practitioners, 2nd rev. ed.* (Thousand Oaks, CA: Corwin Press, 2007).

3. 20 U.S.C. § 1412(a)(1)(B)(i)(ii).

4. 20 U.S.C. § 1401 (3) offers the following definition:

> (3) Child with a disability—
> (A) In general
> The term *child with a disability* means a child—
> (i) with mental retardation, hearing impairments (including deafness), speech or language impairments, visual impairments (including blindness), serious emotional disturbance (hereinafter referred to as "emotional disturbance"), orthopedic impairments, autism, traumatic brain injury, other health impairments, or specific learning disabilities; and
> (ii) who, by reason thereof, needs special education and related services.
> (B) Child aged 3 through 9
> The term *child with a disability* for a child aged 3 through 9 may, at the discretion of the State and the local educational agency, include a child—experiencing developmental delays, as defined by the State and as measured by appropriate diagnostic instruments and procedures, in 1 or more of the following areas: physical development, cognitive development, communication development, social or emotional development, or adaptive development; and
> (ii) who, by reason thereof, needs special education and related services.

5. 20 U.S.C. § 1401(3)(A)(ii).

6. 20 U.S.C. § 1401(26), 34 C.F.R. § 300.34.

7. 20 U.S.C. § 1401(9) Free appropriate public education:

> The term *free appropriate public education* means special education and related services that—
> (A) have been provided at public expense, under public supervision and direction, and without charge;
> (B) meet the standards of the State educational agency;
> (C) include an appropriate preschool, elementary, or secondary school education in the State involved; and
> (D) are provided in conformity with the individualized education program required under section 1414(d).

8. 20 U.S.C. §§ 1401(14), 1414(d). *See* 34 C.F.R. §§ 300.320-328 for additional details on IEPs.

9. 20 U.S.C. § 1401(14).
10. 20 U.S.C.A. § 1414(d)(1)(A).
11. 20 U.S.C.A. § 1402 (3)(A) (ii), 26.
12. 20 U.S.C.A. § 1415.
13. The IDEA's expanded definition of *parent* covers natural, adoptive, or foster parents, guardians, and individuals acting in the place of natural or adoptive parents (including grandparents, stepparents, or other relatives) with whom children live, or individuals who are legally responsible for a child's welfare. 20 U.S.C. § 1401(23).
14. 20 U.S.C.A. § 1414(a)(1)(D)(i)(I).
15. 20 U.S.C.A. § 1414(a)(1)(C)(i)(I).
16. 20 U.S.C.A. § 1414(a)(1)(D)(I).
17. 20 U.S.C.A. § 1414(d)(1)(B)(i).
18. 20 U.S.C.A. § 1414(d)(1)(A).
19. 20 U.S.C.A. § 1414(d)(1)(A)(i)(IV).
20. 20 U.S.C.A. § 1414(d)(1)(A)(I).
21. 34 C.F.R. § 300.323(c)(1).
22. 34 C.F.R. § 300.323(c)(2).
23. 34 C.F.R. § 300.321(a).
24. 34 C.F.R. § 300.325(a)(2).
25. 20 U.S.C.A. § 1415.
26. 34 C.F.R. § 300.140(a).
27. 29 U.S.C.A. § 1232g.
28. 34 C.F.R. §§ 99.1-67.
29. 34 C.F.R. §§ 300.610-627.
30. 34 C.F.R. § 99.1(b). According to 34 C.F.R. § 99.1(a) "(a) Except as otherwise noted in § 99.10, this part applies to an educational agency or institution to which funds have been made available under any program administered by the Secretary, if—

> (1) The educational institution provides educational services or instruction, or both, to students; or
> (2) The educational agency is authorized to direct and control public elementary or secondary, or postsecondary educational institutions."

31. 20 U.S.C.A. § 1415(b)(3)(A).
32. 20 U.S.C.A. § 1414(d)(4).
33. 20 U.S.C.A. § 1414(a)(2)(A).
34. 20 U.S.C.A. § 1415(m)(1).
35. 20 U.S.C.A. § 1415(m)(2).
36. 20 U.S.C.A. § 1414(d)(4).
37. 20 U.S.C.A. § 1414(a)(2)(B)(ii).
38. 20 U.S.C.A. § 1414(d)(1)(A)(I).
39. 20 U.S.C.A. § 1414(d)(5)(A). Related provisions seek to reduce the amount of paperwork associated with the delivery of special education by permitting up to fifteen

states to pilot paperwork-reduction plans to reduce the burden on teachers, administrators, and related service providers. 20 U.S.C.A. §§ 1408(2)(A), 1414(d)(5)(B)(i).

40. 20 U.S.C.A. § 1414(f).

41. 20 U.S.C.A. §§ 1414(d)(1)(A)(VII)(ii), 1401(30).

42. 20 U.S.C.A. § 1415(b)(3)(A).

43. 20 U.S.C.A. § 1415(b)(1).

44. 20 U.S.C.A. § 1415(b)(1).

45. 34 C.F.R. § 300.502(b).

46. 34 C.F.R. § 300.115. In practice, the range of options moves from full inclusion in a regular education classroom, to inclusion with supplementary assistance such as an aide, to partial inclusion, partial resource room placement, to an individualized placement in a resource room, to a special day school, to hospital or homebound instruction, to a residential placement. Typically, the first four options are offered in a child's local school.

47. 34 C.F.R. §§ 300.154(d)-(g).

48. 20 U.S.C.A. §§ 1402 (14), 1414(d).

49. 458 U.S. 176 (1982).

50. For an in-depth analysis of the case and individuals involved, *see* R. C. Smith, *A Case About Amy* (Philadelphia: Temple University Press, 1996).

51. Smith, at 200.

52. *Pink v. Mt. Diablo Unified School Dist.*, 738 F. Supp. 345 (N.D. Cal. 1990).

53. *Nelson v. Southfield Pub. Schools*, 384 N.W.2d 423 (Mich. Ct. App. 1986); *Barwacz v. Michigan Dep't of Educ.*, 681 F. Supp. 427 (W.D. Mich. 1988).

54. *Lagares v. Camdenton R–III School Dist.*, 68 S.W.3d 518 (Mo. Ct. App. 2001).

55. *Geis v. Board of Educ. of Parsippany–Troy Hills*, 774 F.2d 575 (3d Cir. 1985).

56. *Burke County Bd. of Educ. v. Denton*, 895 F.2d 973 (4th Cir.1990); *CM ex rel. JM v. Board of Educ. of Henderson County*, 85 F. Supp.2d 574 (W.D.N.C.1999), *aff'd in part, rev'd and rem'd in part*, 241 F.3d 374 (4th Cir.2001), *on remand*, 184 F. Supp.2d 466 (W.D.N.C.2002).

57. *Va. Code Annotated* § 18–20–5(3).

58. For a more detailed discussion of the refinement of the *Rowley* standard *see* Allan G. Osborne Jr., "Legal Standards for an Appropriate Education in the Post-Rowley Era." 58 *Exceptional Children* 488 (1992).

59. *Hall v. Vance County Board of Educ.*, 774 F.2d 629 (4th Cir. 1985); *Carter v. Florence County School District Four*, 950 F.2d 156 (4th Cir. 1991), *aff'd on other grounds*, 510 U.S. 7 (1993).

60. *Board of Educ. of East Windsor Reg'l School Dist. v. Diamond*, 808 F.2d 987 (3d Cir. 1986); *Polk v. Susquehanna Intermediate Unit 16*, 853 F.2d 171 (3d Cir. 1988).

61. *Chris C. v. Gwinnett County School Dist.*, 780 F. Supp. 804 (N.D. Ga. 1991).

62. *J.S.K. v. Hendry County School Board*, 941 F.2d 1563 (11th Cir. 1991).

63. Perhaps the most significant case on "zero-reject" is *Timothy W. v. Rochester, N.H., School Dist.*, 875 F.2d 954 (1st Cir. 1989), *cert. denied* 493 U.S. 983 (1989) (finding that since there was no requirement in the IDEA that a child with a disability could

benefit from special education in order to be eligible under the IDEA, a board was required to pay for the residential placement of a child with multiple disabilities who was also profoundly mentally retarded).

64. 20 U.S.C.A. §§ 1406(b)(2), 1412(a)(5).

65. 995 F.2d 1204 (3d Cir. 1993).

66. This test was originally proposed in *Daniel R.R. v. State Bd. of Educ.*, 874 F.2d 1036 (5th Cir. 1989).

67. 14 F.3d 1398 (9th Cir. 1994).

68. *See, e.g., Clyde K. v. Puyallup School Dist. No. 3*, 35 F.3d 1396 (9th Cir. 1994); *Capistrano Unified School Dist. v. Wartenberg*, 59 F.3d 884 (9th Cir. 1995).

69. 34 C.F.R. § 300.115.

70. 20 U.S.C.A. § 1412(a)(10)(B).

71. *See, e.g., Colin K. v. Schmidt*, 715 F.2d 1 (1st Cir. 1983).

72. *Gladys J. v. Pearland Indep. School Dist.*, 520 F. Supp. 869 (S.D. Tex. 1981).

73. *Chris D. v. Montgomery County Bd. of Educ.*, 743 F. Supp. 1524 (M.D. Ala. 1990).

74. *Abrahamson v. Hershman*, 701 F.2d F.2d F.2d 223 (1st Cir. 1983).

75. *Parks v. Pavkovic*, 753 F.2d 1397 (7th Cir.1985).

76. *McKenzie v. Jefferson*, EHLR 554:338 (D.D.C. 1983).

77. *Patricia P. v. Board of Educ. of Oak Park and River Forest High School Dist. No. 200*, 203 F.3d 462 (7th Cir. 2000).

78. *Nein v. Greater Clark County School Corp.*, 95 F. Supp.2d 961 (S.D. Ind. 2000).

79. 20 U.S.C.A. § 1412(a)(1), 34 C.F.R. § 300.106.

80. *Armstrong v. Kline*, 476 F. Supp. 583 (E.D. Pa. 1979), *rem'd sub nom. Battle v. Commonwealth of Pa.*, 629 F.2d 269 (3d Cir. 1980), *on remand* 513 F. Supp. 425 (E.D. Pa. 1981), *Cordrey v. Euckert*, 917 F.2d 1460 (6th Cir. 1990).

81. *Anderson v. Thompson*, 658 F.2d 1205 (7th Cir. 1981).

82. 34 C.F.R. § 300.111.

83. 34 C.F.R. § 131(a)).

84. 20 U.S.C.A. § 1401(26).

85. 20 U.S.C.A. § 1412 (a)(10)(A)(I); 34 C.F.R. § 300.131(a).

86. 34 C.F.R. § 300.131(b)(2).

87. 34 C.F.R. § 300.131(c).

88. 20 U.S.C.A. § 1412(a)(16).

89. 20 U.S.C.A. §§ 6301, 6311, 6312, 6316.

90. *Debra P. v. Turlington*, 730 F.2d 1405 (11th Cir. 1984). *See also Anderson v. Banks*, 520 F. Supp. 472 (S.D. Ga. 1981), *modified*, 540 F. Supp. 761 (S.D. Ga. 1982), *appeal dismissed sub. nom., Johnson v. Sikes*, 730 F.2d 644 (11th Cir. 1984) (upholding the use of the California Achievement Test where school officials were able to provide empirical data to support a claim of instructional validity in a district that had operated under de jure segregation); *Board of Educ. of Northport-East Northport Union Free School Dist. v. Ambach*, 458 N.Y.S.2d 680 (N.Y. App. Div. 1982) (upholding minimum

competency testing without having to prove instructional validity because, unlike *Debra P.* and *Anderson*, no prior de jure race discrimination occurred).

91. 20 U.S.C.A. § 1412(a)(6)(B), 34 C.F.R. § 300.304.

92. *Debra P. v. Turlington*, 730 F.2d 1405 (11th Cir. 1984).

93. *Debra P.*, *id.* (striking down testing on the basis that thirteen-month notice was insufficient); *but see Brookhart v. Illinois State Board of Educ.*, 697 F.2d 179 (7th Cir. 1983) (although unwilling to define adequate notice in terms of a specific number of years, the court ruled that by changing a diploma requirement and by providing only one and one-half years' notice for students to prepare for a minimum competency test, school officials deprived failing students of both property and liberty rights; further, the court stipulated that a school board must ensure that students with disabilities be exposed to most of the test material or show that a well-informed decision was made not to pursue an MCT-based program); *Anderson v. Banks*, 520 F. Supp. 472 (S.D. Ga. 1981), *modified* 540 F. Supp. 761 (S.D. Ga. 1982) (holding that twenty-four-month notice was sufficient due to the presumed general applicability of the California Achievement Test (CAT), the availability of remedial alternatives, and the ease of coordinating activities in a single district).

94. *Brookhart v. Illinois State Bd. of Educ.*, 697 F.2d 179 (7th Cir. 1983).

95. 28 IDELR 1002 (1998).

96. 20 U.S.C.A. § 1414(d)(1)(B)(i).

97. 20 U.S.C.A. § 1401(a)(26).

98. 20 U.S.C.A. § 1401(26)(B).

99. 468 U.S. 883 (1984).

100. 526 U.S. 66 (1999).

101. For more detailed discussions of this case and its implications, *see* Charles J. Russo, "*Cedar Rapids Community School District v. Garret T.*: School Districts Must Pay for Nursing Services Under the IDEA," 65 *School Business Affairs, No.* 6, 35 (1999) and Allan G. Osborne, "Supreme Court Rules That Schools Must Provide Full-Time Nursing Services for Medically Fragile Students," 136 *Education Law Reporter* 1 (1999).

102. 20 U.S.C.A. § 1401(A), 34 C.F.R. § 300.5.

103. 20 U.S.C.A. § 1401(A).

104. 20 U.S.C.A. § 1401(2), 34 C.F.R. § 300.6.

105. *Oberti v. Board of Educ. of the Borough of Clementon School District*, 995 F.2d 1204 (3d Cir. 1993).

106. 34 C.F.R. § 300.324(a)(2)(v).

107. 34 C.F.R. § 300.105(a).

108. 34 C.F.R. § 300.105(b).

109. 64 *Fed. Reg.* 12406 *et seq.* at 12591 (March 12, 1999).

110. 64 *Fed. Reg.* at 12540.

111. 20 U.S.C.A. § 1415(i)(2); 34 C.F.R. § 300.516(c)(3).

112. 20 U.S.C.A. § 1415(e).

113. 20 U.S.C.A. § 1415(f)(1)(B)(i); 34 C.F.R. § 300.510(a).

114. For a discussion of resolution sessions and their mandatory nature *see* Allan G. Osborne and Charles J. Russo, "Resolution Sessions Under the IDEA: Are They Mandatory?" 218 *Education Law Reporter* 7 (2007).

115. 20 U.S.C.A. § 1415(e)(2)(B).

116. 20 U.S.C.A. § 1415(f).

117. 20 U.S.C.A. § 1415(i)(2)(A).

118. 20 U.S.C.A. § 1415(j).

119. 20 U.S.C.A. § 1415(k)(2).

120. *Honig v. Doe*, 484 U.S. 305 (1988).

121. 20 U.S.C.A. § 1415(i)(2)(B).

122. *Board of Educ. of Hendrick Hudson Cent. School Dist. v. Rowley*, 458 U.S. 176, 208 (1982). According to the Court, "[w]e previously have cautioned that courts lack the 'specialized knowledge and experience' necessary to resolve 'persistent and difficult questions of educational policy. . . . Therefore, once a court determines that the requirements of the Act have been met, questions of methodology are for resolution by the States [through school officials.]" Internal citations omitted).

123. 20 U.S.C.A. § 1415(f)(3)(C).

124. 20 U.S.C.A. § 1415(f)(3)(D).

125. 20 U.S.C.A. § 1415(l).

126. 42 U.S.C.A. § 1983.

127. *See, e.g., Marvin H. v. Austin Indep. School District*, 714 F.2d 1348 (5th Cir. 1983).

128. *See, e.g., Ft. Zumwalt School District v. Missouri State Board of Educ.*, 865 F. Supp. 604 (E.D. Mo. 1994).

129. For a discussion of damages in special education, *see* Allan G. Osborne Jr. and Charles J. Russo, "Are Damages an Available Remedy When a School District Fails to Provide an Appropriate Education under IDEA?" 152 *Education Law Reporter* 1 (2001).

130. *See, e.g., W.B. v. Matula*, 67 F.3d 484 (3d Cir. 1995); *Whitehead v. School District for Hillsborough County*, 918 F. Supp. 1515 (M.D. Fla. 1996). *But see A.W. v. Jersey City Pub. Schs.*, 486 F.3d 791 (3d Cir. 2007) where the Third Circuit effectively abrogated its previous ruling in *W.B. v. Matula* by holding that Section 1983 could not be used to remedy violations of the IDEA. As of this writing the courts are split on the question. For a discussion of this topic *see* Allan G. Osborne, "Can Section 1983 Be Used to Redress Violations of the IDEA: An Update," 230 *Education Law Reporter* 453 (2008).

131. 471 U.S. 359 (1985).

132. 510 U.S. 7 (1993).

133. *Gagliardo v. Arlington Cent. School Dist.*, 489 F.3d 105 (2d Cir. 2007). *See also Pinn ex rel. Steven P. v. Harrison Cent. School Dist.*, 473 F. Supp.2d 477 (S.D.N.Y. 2007) (parents failed to demonstrate that the private school was appropriate), *Matrejek v. Brewster Cent. School Dist.*, 471 F. Supp.2d 415 (S.D.N.Y. 2007) (student made no

forward progress in the private school and the school did not have a plan for addressing his problems), *Berger v. Medina City School Dist.*, 348 F.3d 513 (6th Cir. 2003) (private sectarian school could not be considered a proper placement where it did not provide some element of the special education services the student required).

134. *Lauren W. ex rel. Jean W. v. DeFlaminis*, 480 F.3d 259 (3d Cir. 2007). *See also Frank G. and Diane G. v. Board of Educ. of Hyde Park*, 459 F.3d 356 (2d Cir. 2006) (reimbursement appropriate for a sectarian private school that offered small class size and a program designed to accommodate the student's needs), *cert. den'd* 128 S. Ct. 436 (2007) (on the narrow question of whether reimbursement was appropriate where the student had never attended the public schools), *Lamoine School Comm. v. Ms. Z.*, 353 F. Supp.2d 18 (D. Me. 2005) (reimbursement granted for a boarding school that was not a special education facility but provided an appropriate education).

135. *See, e.g., Frank G. and Diane G. v. Board of Educ. of Hyde Park*, supra n. 200, *N.G. v. District of Columbia*, 556 F. Supp.2d 11 (D.D.C. 2008) (tuition awarded for placements in both a sectarian and non-sectarian school that provided an appropriate placement).

136. *Matthew J. v. Massachusetts Dep't of Educ.*, 989 F. Supp. 380 (D. Mass. 1998).

137. *See for example, L.M. ex rel. H.M. v. Evesham Township Bd. of Educ.*, 256 F. Supp.2d 290 (D.N.J. 2003) (state law did not bar tuition reimbursement at a sectarian school where the public school board's proposed IEP was deemed to have been inappropriate).

138. *See, e.g., Lester H. v. Gilhool*, 916 F.2d 865 (3d Cir. 1990); *Todd D. v. Andrews*, 933 F.2d 1576 (11th Cir. 1991); *Manchester School District v. Christopher B.*, 807 F. Supp. 860 (D.N.H. 1992).

139. *See, e.g., Valerie J. v. Derry Cooperative School District*, 771 F. Supp. 483 (D.N.H. 1991); *Big Beaver Falls Area School District v. Jackson*, 624 A.2d 806 (Pa. Commw. Ct. 1993).

140. *See, e.g., Pihl v. Massachusetts Dep't of Educ.*, 9 F.3d 184 (1st Cir. 1993); *Jones v. Schneider*, 896 F. Supp. 488 (D.V.I. 1995).

141. *Draper v. Atlanta Indep. School System*, 518 F.3d 1275 (11th Cir. 2008).

142. *Smith v. Robinson*, 468 U.S. 992 (1984).

143. 20 U.S.C.A. § 1415(i)(3), 34 C.F.R. § 300.517.

144. *See, e.g., Verginia M.C. v. Corrigan-Camden Indep. School Dist.*, 909 F. Supp. 1023 (E.D. Tex. 1995).

145. *Howie v. Tippecanoe School Corp.*, 734 F. Supp. 1485 (N.D. Ind. 1990).

146. *Beard v. Teska*, 31 F.3d 942 (10th Cir. 1994).

147. *Mr. D. v. Glocester School Comm.*, 711 F. Supp. 66 (D.R.I. 1989); *Hall v. Detroit Pub. School*, 823 F. Supp. 1377 (E.D. Mich.1993).

148. *See Woodside v. School Dist. of Philadelphia Bd. of Educ.*, 248 F.3d 129 (3d Cir. 2001); *Erickson v. Board of Educ. of Baltimore County*, 162 F.3d 289 (4th Cir. 1998).

149. 548 U.S.291 (2006).

150. For a lengthier discussion of this topic, *see* Allan G. Osborne Jr. and C. J. Russo, *Discipline of Students with Disabilities: Legal Issues* (Thousand Oaks, CA: Corwin Press, 2009).

151. The procedures for disciplining students in regular education were spelled out for the first time in *Goss v. Lopez*, 419 U.S. 565 (1975).

152. *See, e.g., S-1 v. Turlington*, 635 F.2d 342 (5th Cir. 1981).

153. 484 U.S. 305 (1988).

154. 20 U.S.C.A. § § 1415(i)(j)(k)(l).

155. 34 C.F.R. § 300.519(a).

156. 34 C.F.R. § 300.520(a)(2).

157. 20 U.S.C.A. § 1415(k)(1), 34 C.F.R. § 300.520.

158. 34 C.F.R. § 300.520(a)(2).

159. 18 U.S.C.A. § 930(g)(2).

160. 20 U.S.C.A. § 1415(k)(7)(B); 34 C.F.R. § 300.530(i)(1). The Controlled Substances Act, 21 U.S.C.A. § 812(c), lists the full categorization of controlled substances.

161. 20 U.S.C.A. § 1415(k)(1)(G)(iii); 34 C.F.R. § 300.530(g)(3).

162. 20 U.S.C.A. § 1415(k)(7)(c); 34 C.F.R. § 300.530(i)(3).

163. 18 U.S.C.A. § 1365(h)(3).

164. 18 U.S.C.A. § 1365(h)(4).

165. 20 U.S.C.A. § 1415(k)(1)(D)(ii).

166. 20 U.S.C.A. §§ 1415(k)(1),(7), 34 C.F.R. § 300.530.

167. 34 C.F.R. § 300.520(b)(1)(ii).

168. 20 U.S.C.A. § 1415(k)(1)(D)(ii); 34 C.F.R. § 300.530(d)(1)(ii).

169. 20 U.S.C.A. § 1415(k)(1)(F)(i); 34 C.F.R. § 300.530(f)(1).

170. 20 U.S.C.A. § 1415(k)(4)(A), 34 C.F.R. § 300.533.

171. 20 U.S.C.A. § 1415(k)(4)(A), 34 C.F.R. § 300.533.

172. 20 U.S.C.A. § 1415(k)(1)(E).

173. 20 U.S.C.A. § 1415(k)(1)(F).

174. 20 U.S.C.A. § 1415(k)(1)(E)(i).

175. 20 U.S.C.A. § 1415(k)(1)(E)(i).

176. 20 U.S.C.A. § 1415(k)(1)(c).

177. 20 U.S.C.A. § 1415(k)(1)(E)(i).

178. 20 U.S.C.A. § 1415(k)(1) (c); 34 C.F.R. § 300.530 (c).

179. 20 U.S.C.A. § 1415(k)(4)(B).

180. 20 U.S.C.A. § 1415(k)(4)(A).

181. *Commonwealth of Va. Dep't of Educ. v. Riley*, 106 F.3d 559 (4th Cir. 1997).

182. 20 U.S.C.A. §1415(k)(1)(D)(i).

183. 34 C.F.R. § 300.121(d)(1).

184. 20 U.S.C.A. § 1415(k)(5).

185. 20 U.S.C.A. § 1415(k)(5)(B), 34 C.F.R. § 300.534(b).

186. 20 U.S.C.A. § 1415(k)(5) (c); 34 C.F.R. § 300.534(c)(2).

187. 20 U.S.C.A. § 1415(k)(5)(C); 34 C.F.R. §§ 300.534(c)(1)-(2).

188. 20 U.S.C.A. § 1415(k)(5)(D)(i); 34 C.F.R. § 300.534(d)(1).

189. 20 U.S.C.A. § 1415(k)(5)(D)(ii); 34 C.F.R. § 300.534(d)(2).
190. 34 C.F.R. § 300.534(d)(2)(ii).
191. 34 C.F.R. § 300.534(d)(2)(iii).
192. 20 U.S.C.A. § 1415(k)(6)(A), 34 C.F.R. § 300.535(a).
193. 20 U.S.C.A. § 1415(k)(6)(B), 34 C.F.R. § 300.535(b).
194. 20 U.S.C.A. § 1232g.

5

THE IDEA AND NON-PUBLIC SCHOOLS

In light of the significant issues that arise for non-public schools, this chapter begins with a brief overview of the lengthy and complex history of litigation involving the acceptable parameters of state aid to non-public schools under the Establishment Clause of the First Amendment. After examining litigation involving the Establishment Clause, the chapter reviews the provisions of the Individuals with Disabilities Education Act (IDEA) that apply to non-public schools and their students. The chapter next considers litigation interpreting the IDEA before discussing topics that present special concerns and the impact of state laws on the rights of students with disabilities who attend non-public schools.

THE ESTABLISHMENT CLAUSE, AID, AND NON-PUBLIC SCHOOLS

According to the Religion Clauses of the First Amendment, which became part of the United States Constitution along with the rest of the Bill of Rights in 1791, "Congress shall make no law respecting an establishment of religion, or prohibiting the free exercise thereof." Based on the many disputes that have been litigated under the First Amendment

Religion Clauses, some background on the Establishment Clause and state aid is necessary in order to appreciate the constitutional dimensions of issues surrounding the status of this complex topic, especially as it relates to religiously affiliated non-public schools and their students.

Controversy over state aid to religiously affiliated non-public schools under the Establishment Clause began in 1947 with the Supreme Court's ruling in *Everson v. Board of Education* (*Everson*).[1] In *Everson* the Court upheld a statute from New Jersey that authorized the reimbursement of parents for the cost of transportation associated with sending their children to religiously affiliated and other types of non-public schools.[2] In so deciding, the Court also enunciated the child benefit test[3] which permits a variety of forms of aid to children in non-public schools, a judicial standard that has had a checkered history.[4]

The second stage of the development of the Supreme Court's Establishment Clause began with the tripartite test that the Justices enunciated in *Lemon v. Kurtzman*.[5] During this time, the Court refused to move beyond the boundaries it had previously set. Under this seemingly ubiquitous standard:

> Every analysis in this area must begin with consideration of the cumulative criteria developed by the Court over many years. Three such tests may be gleaned from our cases. First, the statute must have a secular legislative purpose; second, its principal or primary effect must be one that neither advances nor inhibits religion; finally, the statute must not foster "an excessive government entanglement with religion."[6]

Perhaps the low point of the child benefit test, from the perspective of its supporters, occurred in 1985 when, in *Aguilar v. Felton*,[7] the Supreme Court banned the on-site delivery of remedial Title I[8] services in religiously affiliated non-public schools. The Court struck down a program in New York City even in the absence of allegations of misconduct or misappropriation of public funds based on the fear that having educators from public schools provide services in religiously affiliated non-public schools might have created "excessive entanglement" between the government and religion. Consequently, since school boards still had to provide services at public schools or neutral sites, many students who attended religiously affiliated non-public schools were denied equal educational opportunities under Title I.[9]

Fortunately, from the point of view of those who are interested in religiously affiliated non-public schools, the landscape with regard to state aid to K–12, education began to evolve[10] in 1993 when the Supreme Court revitalized the child benefit test in *Zobrest v. Catalina Foothills School District* (*Zobrest*).[11] In *Zobrest* the Court ruled that the Establishment Clause did not bar a public school district in Arizona from providing the on-site delivery of the services of a sign-language interpreter for a student who attended a Roman Catholic high school. The Court reasoned that since the interpreter was essentially a conduit through whom information passed, the on-site delivery of such assistance did not violate the Establishment Clause.[12]

Four years later, in *Agostini v. Felton* (*Agostini*),[13] the Court virtually lifted the ban against the on-site delivery of services to students who attended religiously affiliated non-public schools in New York City as long as appropriate safeguards were in place.[14] Most recently, in *Mitchell v. Helms*,[15] a suit from Louisiana, the Supreme Court,[16] in a plurality opinion upheld the constitutionality of Chapter 2, now Title VI, of Title I of the Elementary and Secondary Education Act,[17] a far-reaching federal statute that permits the loan of state-owned instructional materials such as computers, slide projectors, television sets, tape recorders, maps, and globes to non-public schools.[18]

The Supreme Court further expanded the boundaries of aid under the Establishment Clause in *Zelman v. Simmons–Harris*.[19] Here the Court upheld the limited use of vouchers for poor children in Cleveland, Ohio, most of whom attended religiously affiliated non-public schools because they were unwelcome in local public schools in neighboring districts.[20]

A major statutory change occurred in 1997 when congressional reauthorization of the IDEA included provisions clarifying the obligations of public school systems to provide special education and related services to students in non-public schools. Unfortunately, neither Congress nor the courts conclusively answered questions about the delivery of special education for children in religiously affiliated non-public schools.

Regulatory modifications that were promulgated in 1999, and extended in the 2006 regulations incident to the 2004 version of the IDEA, created a dilemma. On the one hand, the IDEA and its regulations make it clear that children in religiously affiliated non-public schools are entitled to receive some special education services. Yet, on the other hand, these same provisions contain funding restrictions that actually mean that students in non-public schools are very likely to receive fewer services[21] in the event that officials in public schools follow the letter of the law and are unable to make additional services available to children who are qualified for special education.

THE IDEA AND NON-PUBLIC SCHOOLS

As noted, the 1997 reauthorization of the IDEA included provisions clarifying the obligations of public school systems to provide special education and related services to students in non-public schools. The 2004 amendments to the IDEA further clarified these parts of the law.[22]

The changes in the IDEA notwithstanding, unfortunately, neither Congress nor the courts conclusively answered questions about the delivery of special education for children in religiously affiliated non-public schools in the 1997 or 2004 amendments. Regulatory modifications that were adopted in 1999, and which changed little in the 2004 amendments, created a dilemma. The regulations, and earlier case law, made it clear that children in religiously affiliated non-public schools were entitled to receive some special education services, but the laws set funding restrictions in place that limited the amount of services that these children can receive on-site in their religious schools. The net result is that these students are likely to receive fewer services if public school officials follow the letter of the law and do not make additional services available to qualified students in religious schools.

According to the IDEA[23] and its regulations,[24] children whose parents voluntarily enroll them in non-public schools are entitled to some level of special education services. Further, the IDEA permits the on-site delivery of special education for students with disabilities whose parents have placed them in "private," schools, including religious, elementary and secondary schools,[25] as long as safeguards are in place to avoid "excessive entanglement" between public school systems and religious institutions. Such an approach is consistent with settled law that public school personnel can conduct diagnostic tests on-site in religiously affiliated non-public schools to evaluate whether children are eligible for services in programs that are supported by public funds.[26]

The regulations incorporate statutory changes and provide guidance on meeting the IDEA's requirements while borrowing from preexisting Education Department General Administrative Regulations (EDGAR).[27] EDGAR requires school boards to provide students in non-public schools with opportunities for equitable participation in federal programs.[28] This means that students in non-public schools are entitled to opportunities to participate in federal programs that are comparable in quality to those available to children in public school.[29] In developing programs, public school personnel must consult with representatives of the non-public schools to consider which students will be served, how their needs will be identified, what benefits they will receive, how the benefits will be delivered, and how the programs will be evaluated.[30]

DEFINITION OF PRIVATE SCHOOL STUDENTS

Public school officials must locate, identify, and evaluate all students with disabilities who attend "private schools" within their jurisdictions, including children whose parents place them in private schools.[31] In other words, officials at public school boards must develop plans to permit these students in non-public schools to participate in programs carried out pursuant to the IDEA.[32] The regulations define students in non-public schools as those whose parents have voluntarily enrolled them in such schools or facilities.[33] This definition does not include students whose school boards have placed them in private facilities at public expense in order to provide each of them with a FAPE.

SPENDING LIMITS

In key language, the IDEA and its regulations set a cap on the amount of money that public school boards must spend in providing services to students whose parents have enrolled them in non-public schools.[34] This total is limited to a proportionate amount of the federal funds that public school boards receive based on the number of students in non-public schools in relation to the overall number of children in their districts.[35] At the same time, nothing prohibits school boards from using state funds to offer more than the IDEA requires insofar as the regulation establishes only a minimum amount that officials must spend on qualified students in non-public schools.[36]

Under the regulations, IDEA funds cannot be used to benefit private schools.[37] Put another way, public funds cannot be used to offer impermissible aid to religious institutions by financing existing instructional programs, otherwise providing them with direct financial benefits such as money, or organizing classes based on students' religions or schools they attend.[38] Even so, the regulations allow boards to employ public school personnel in these non-public schools as long as they are not supplanting services that are normally provided by those institutions.[39] The regulations further permit boards to hire personnel from non-public schools to provide services outside of their regular hours of work as long as they are under the supervision and control of officials from the public schools.[40] Finally, any property, equipment, or supplies purchased with IDEA funds can only be used on-site in non-public schools for the benefit of students with disabilities.[41]

COMPARABLE SERVICES

The IDEA's regulations specify that students who attend private schools do not have an individual right to receive some or all of the special education and related services that they might have received in public schools.[42] This does not mean that children in private schools are denied all services under the IDEA.[43] Instead, the regulations grant public school officials the authority to develop service plans and to decide which students from private schools will be served.[44]

In a related provision, the IDEA requires public school officials to ensure that representatives of private or religious schools have the opportunity to attend such meetings. To this end, the IDEA includes language that such sessions should have the parties engage in "timely and meaningful consultation"[45] with public officials or allow them to participate by other means such as individual or conference calls.[46] In addition, the IDEA directs local public school officials to obtain written affirmation from educators in non-public schools confirming that they engaged in the required "timely and meaningful consultation."[47] Officials in non-public schools can file complaints with state-level agencies if public school officials failed to engage in appropriate consultations or did not give appropriate consideration to their points of view.[48]

Students in non-public schools are entitled to receive services from personnel who meet the same standards as educators in public schools,[49] even if they receive a different, lesser[50] amount of services than their peers in public schools.[51] Insofar as students with disabilities who attend non-public schools are not entitled to the same amount of services as similarly situated students who attend public schools, the regulations do not require the development of an IEP. Instead, the regulations require school officials to develop service plans describing the aid that they will provide to students.[52] Even so, service plans must not only meet the same content requirements as IEPs but must also be developed, reviewed, and revised in a manner consistent with the IEP process.[53]

DELIVERY OF SERVICES

The regulations reiterate that public school boards can provide special education and related services that are "secular, neutral, and non-ideological"[54] on-site in non-public schools.[55] At the same time, the IDEA specifies that school boards can provide related services using their own personnel or by means of contracts with private individuals or groups.[56]

In order to differentiate between public and private schools, the regulations specifically use the term *including religious schools* to reflect the fact that religiously affiliated non-public schools are included within the IDEA's framework.[57]

If it is necessary for children to benefit from services that are not offered on-site and students must be transported to alternate locations to receive them, school boards must provide transportation between their schools or home to sites where they receive services[58] and from the service sites to their non-public schools or homes, depending on the time of day.[59] At the same time, school boards are not required to transport private school students from their homes to their private schools.[60] In a significant addition with potentially far-reaching financial ramifications, it is important to recognize that the cost of transportation may be included in calculating the minimum amount of federal funds that school boards must spend on students in non-public schools.[61]

DISPUTE RESOLUTION

The IDEA's procedural safeguards generally do not apply to complaints that school board officials failed to deliver services to students in non-public schools.[62] The due process provisions do apply to complaints that boards failed to comply with the child find requirements applicable to students in non-public schools[63] and to complaints pursuant to allegations arising in connection with state administration of special education.[64]

In a provision that heightens the protection available for students in non-public schools, the IDEA requires the federal Secretary of Education, under so-called by-pass provisions, to ensure the delivery of special education services for eligible children if state or local school officials either substantially fail in their duty to do so or are unwilling to provide services.[65] In addition to describing how these services are to be paid for,[66] this so-called by-pass part of the law also stipulates that the Secretary cannot act on complaints until state officials have had at least forty-five days to respond to charges that students were not served.[67]

CHILD FIND

The 2004 modification of the IDEA and its regulations require officials in public schools to identify children with disabilities whose parents enrolled them in private schools (including religious, elementary, and secondary schools) in their districts rather than simply those who live within school districts.[68] Under these provisions, officials in public schools must provide accurate counts to state education agencies of the number of children from non-public schools whom they had evaluated, determined to have had disabilities, and served.[69]

The changes also require school board officials to use child find activities for students in private schools that are similar to those used to identify children who attend public schools.[70] Moreover, the cost of such activities does not count in calculating whether school systems exceeded the amount that they spent in serving students who attend private schools.[71]

LITIGATION INVOLVING STUDENTS IN NON-PUBLIC SCHOOLS

As often as the IDEA has been litigated, it is surprising that so relatively few of the cases contested the delivery of special education for students whose parents voluntarily enrolled them in religiously affiliated non-public schools. Even though the recent statutory and regulatory changes address many of the issues that were already litigated, a review of relevant litigation involving the IDEA and non-public schools can be helpful to readers who might be faced with similar situations.

The cases in this section focus on two primary issues involving non-public schools, the on-site delivery of services and the availability of due process procedures to students and their parents. In examining these cases, readers should recognize that insofar as the issues in disputes over special education placements overlap significantly, many of these cases could be listed under either or both headings.

ON-SITE DELIVERY OF SERVICES

A major controversy that the 1997 IDEA Amendments seem to have resolved is whether school boards are obligated to provide special education on-site at religiously affiliated non-public schools. In a case from Virginia, the Fourth Circuit initially held that a school board met its obligation under the IDEA by offering such services at a local public school rather than the Christian school that the student attended.[72] Following *Zobrest*,[73] the Fourth Circuit affirmed its earlier judgment that the services did not have to be provided on-site.[74]

Four other courts agreed with the Fourth Circuit.[75] These courts generally ruled that school boards met their obligations under the IDEA when services were made available to children at public schools. Yet, not all courts agreed, as others interpreted the regulations as requiring boards to provide students in non-public schools with services that were comparable in quality, scope, and opportunity to those offered to their peers in public schools.[76] Insofar as three of these cases were appealed to the Supreme Court,[77] they are discussed in the following paragraphs.

If school boards do not provide services on-site, the question arises as to whether they can be required to offer transportation to students between non-public schools and the locations where they received services.[78] Even though a regulation specifically addresses this question by declaring that transportation must be provided if students need it to benefit from or participate in the special education programs, litigation has ensued.[79]

In a case from Missouri, a federal trial court reasoned that a school board had to provide a student with visual and mobility impairments transportation from the sidewalk in front of her religiously affiliated non-public school to the public school where she attended special education classes.[80] Conversely, the Eleventh Circuit, in a judgment from Alabama that was rendered shortly after the passage of the 1997 IDEA Amendments, but that involved a situation that occurred prior to its enactment, found that a school board was not required to transport a student who attended an Episcopalian school to a public school for speech therapy.[81] Although acknowledging that transportation was a related service, the court concluded that it was unnecessary since the student could walk safely from one school site to the other. These cases can be reconciled because in the case from Alabama, the student was able to access services without transportation, while in Missouri the child's disabilities prevented her from taking advantage of the services without transportation between sites.

As appeals in the three cases identified earlier were pending before the Supreme Court,[82] Congress passed the 1997 IDEA Amendments. Subsequently, the Court vacated these cases and returned the disputes to the lower courts for reconsideration in light of the Amendments. On remand, the courts had to consider what the school boards had to do both prior to and after the adoption of the 1997 IDEA Amendments because even though the suits arose before the changes were passed, the students continued to need special education.

In the case from Indiana, the Seventh Circuit originally denied the request of a student for an instructional aide on-site in her Catholic school.[83] On remand from the Supreme Court, the Seventh Circuit affirmed that the 1997 IDEA Amendments did not require states and school boards to spend their money to ensure that students with disabilities who attend non-public schools would receive publicly funded special education comparable with what is offered to children in public schools.[84]

A related dispute arose in Wisconsin where a federal trial court, citing the case from Indiana, asserted that a student who was hearing impaired whose parents enrolled him in a Christian school was not entitled to the services of a sign-language interpreter.[85] In decreeing that the 1997 IDEA Amendments confirmed that an interpreter did not have to be provided on-site in the religious school, the court wrote that the local school board complied with the law by offering a FAPE at a public school. The court was of the view that when the parents rejected the public school placement that offered an appropriate education, they elected a lesser entitlement for their son.

In a case that was resolved prior to the enactment of the IDEA Amendments, the Tenth Circuit originally indicated that a school board in Kansas was not required to provide a sign-language interpreter on-site at a private nonsectarian school if doing so cost more than delivering a similar service at a public school.[86] On remand, the Tenth Circuit determined that since the 1997 IDEA Amendments were not applicable retroactively, its original judgment stood with respect to events that took place before they went into effect on June 4, 1997.[87] Conversely, as to actions after June 4, 1997, the court explained that the school board's sole obligation was to spend a proportionate amount of federal funds on students in non-public schools. The court remarked that the IDEA Amendments did not require states and local school boards to spend their own funds to provide special education for children whose parents voluntarily enrolled them in non-public schools. The court was satisfied that school boards merely had to make a proportionate amount of federal funds available to pay for the education of children who attended non-public schools.

The Second Circuit, in a case from New York, initially declared that if delivering special education services at a Roman Catholic school entailed significant additional costs, a school board would have complied with the IDEA by offering them at a local public school.[88] On remand, the Second Circuit agreed that the 1997 IDEA Amendments did not require school boards to spend their own funds on students with disabilities whose parents voluntarily enrolled them in non-public schools.[89] Instead, the court was of the opinion that school boards were only required to offer services that can be paid for with a proportionate amount of the federal IDEA funds. The court reiterated that the IDEA does not obligate boards to deliver on-site services to students with disabilities whose parents voluntarily enroll them in non-public schools since the language of the Act is permissive rather than mandatory.

When the Second Circuit returned the litigation to a federal trial court, it issued yet another judgment in this long-standing dispute over the rights of a student who was mentally retarded to receive special education services on-site at her Catholic school.[90] The court declared that the school board was not required to provide the student with the necessary services on-site because insofar as the provision of the requested services was permissive, rather than compulsory, under the 1997 version of the IDEA, school officials were free to act as they did.

In a case from Louisiana, the Fifth Circuit initially held that a hearing-impaired student in a Catholic school was entitled to the on-site delivery of the assistance of a speech and language interpreter if he could demonstrate that he had a genuine need for such aid.[91] After withdrawing its original opinion in light of the passage of the 1997 IDEA Amendments, the court reversed itself in finding that the board was not required to furnish the student with an interpreter since his parents rejected its offer of a FAPE at a public school.[92]

The first of three cases from the Eighth Circuit was a dispute from Missouri that was resolved shortly after the 1997 IDEA Amendments went into effect. Here a student in a Catholic school was denied the on-site delivery of special education services because the court was satisfied that the local school board met its obligation by offering them at a public school. In the first, the Eighth Circuit affirmed its pre-Amendment decision but relied on the revised version of the IDEA since the child and her parents sought prospective relief.[93] The court contended that under the amended IDEA, the student did not have an individual right to receive special education at a particular location.

In a case from Minnesota, the Eighth Circuit ruled that a child in a Christian school did not have a right to the on-site delivery of services from a full-time paraprofessional.[94] Yet, since the school board had a long-standing policy and practice of providing services to students with disabilities at nonreligious, non-public, and home schools, the court reasoned that the denial of similar services to a student in a religiously affiliated school amounted to religious discrimination. The court added that under *Agostini*, the board lacked a valid argument that it risked violating the Establishment Clause by delivering special education at the religious school.

On remand, the federal trial court acknowledged that since the board violated the pre-Amendment version of the IDEA by refusing to provide the child with the services he needed unless he attended a public school, he was entitled to prospective relief.[95] In other words, the court concluded that since school officials violated the child's rights under the IDEA, he was entitled to the services of a full-time paraprofessional for the next six years regardless of where he attended school.

In a case from Rhode Island, a student from a religious school initially received special education services on-site from a public school teacher. When she changed schools, the local school committee (as school boards are called in most New England states) chose to discontinue the on-site delivery of services. However, the school committee did offer to make services available at an off-site location. A hearing officer maintained that the school committee was required to create an IEP for the student taking into consideration that she may receive services at her present religious school.

When the school committee filed suit, the federal trial court ruled that officials were not required to provide the on-site delivery of services.[96] The court thought that the IDEA and its regulations clearly gave the school committee the full authority, and discretion, to provide on-site services at all of the religious schools in the district, some of them, or none at all. However, the court added that the public schools should have conducted an IEP meeting when the student changed schools.

RIGHT TO SERVICES

Where a student in New York with a severe communication and speech disorder spent most of her elementary school years in a communication disorder program operated by an intermediate unit, as she entered the sixth grade officials recommended that she attend a program in a middle school. After two years of disagreements with school officials over the most appropriate placement for their daughter, the parents unilaterally enrolled her in a private school that was not approved by the state for special education along with seeking a hearing. The parties resolved this phase of their dispute by entering into a settlement agreement that provided, among other things, tuition reimbursement. A year later another disagreement developed when the school board officials recommended that the child be placed in a program in an intermediate unit. When the parents rejected this proposal, they left their daughter in the private school. A hearing officer ordered the board to reimburse the parents for private school tuition but a state reviewing officer reversed the decision.

After exhausting administrative remedies, a federal trial court agreed that the private school was the student's status quo placement pending resolution of the dispute and that it offered an appropriate placement.[97] Still, the court held that the student was not entitled to related services since the IDEA limits the rights of students in private schools to receive related services. The court found that the IDEA's regulations specifically stated that the Act's due process procedures are inapplicable to failures by local school officials to provide students in private schools with related services. The court noted that the regulations did not make an exception for children who were placed in private schools only because their boards were unable to provide them with a FAPE in public school settings. Insofar as neither the IDEA nor its regulations conferred a right to a hearing if related services were not provided, the court concluded that no right to related services existed.

LOCATION OF SERVICES

In Delaware, a student who was hearing impaired attended the state school for the deaf through the fifth grade. At that time, his parents requested that he be mainstreamed into classes at a religiously affiliated non-public school and be provided with a sign-language interpreter. School officials responded that they would provide the sign-language interpreter only if the student enrolled in a public school. When the parents disagreed, a hearing panel found that the board had no duty to fund the student's placement at the religious school but officials exercised their discretion properly by declining to provide the student with the sign-language interpreter. When the case went to court, the federal trial court overturned the hearing panel's adjudication as erroneous as a matter of law.[98]

According to the court, since the school board provided a FAPE but the parents elected to place the child in a religious school, it was not liable for the cost of the child's education, including special education and related services. The court noted that the cost of the sign-language interpreter would be more than ten times the amount available for all parentally-placed students in non-public schools in the district. Based not only on this cost element but also on the fact that IDEA does not impose obligations on public school boards to provide related services on individualized bases to parentally-placed students in non-public schools, the court concluded that the hearing panel's decision was incorrect.

The Eighth Circuit ruled that under the 1997 IDEA Amendments, since a child from Nebraska whose parents unilaterally enrolled him in a private residential facility lacked an individual right to special education and related services, there was no basis on which the family could seek a court order mandating the delivery of services at a particular location.[99] The court pointed out that the child, who was severely disabled and needed constant medical attention, was not entitled to receive special education services at the licensed nursing facility where he had been placed by his parents. Prior to being placed in the nursing facility, the student had received the requested services at home.

DISPUTE RESOLUTION

In a case from New Hampshire that began before the 2004 Amendments came into effect, the parents of a student who attended a religiously affiliated non-public school but received special education services from the public school system unsuccessfully requested a due process hearing. The parents made this request because they were dissatisfied with the services that their son received. In denying the request the hearing officer explained that neither the IDEA nor state law entitled the parents to a hearing unless their son was enrolled in a public school. In their suit challenging the hearing officer's adjudication, the parents alleged that the IDEA impermissibly burdened their right to send their child to a religious school, denied them a suitable forum to litigate their dispute, and penalized them for their choosing to send the child to a religiously affiliated non-public school.

The federal trial court agreed that the student was not entitled to a hearing because insofar as children with disabilities in non-public schools lack individually enforceable rights to receive special education and related services, the IDEA does not grant their parents the right to due process hearings. Instead, the court acknowledged that states must adopt procedures for resolving such parental complaints, a limitation that followed logically from the congressional determination that students in non-public schools did not have individually enforceable rights to services. The court added that the disputed IDEA provisions are not improperly coercive because they did not place undue pressure on the parents' right to send their child to a private school.

On further review, the First Circuit affirmed that the benefits that the student and his parents sought were benefits earmarked for those who were enrolled in public schools.[100] Those benefits, the court declared, would have been available to the student if he had attended a public school. The court observed that parents who choose to send their children to non-public schools have no legitimate expectancy that their children will receive the same federal or state financial benefits that they would have been afforded had they attended public schools.

SPECIAL CONCERNS

As significant as the litigation surrounding the IDEA has been, at least four important issues still remain in need of some additional clarification about the delivery of special education for children in non-public schools: whether services must be provided to all students whose parents voluntarily enroll them in religious schools; whether public school officials have discretion over where and how services are delivered; whether boards must offer services to children whose parents voluntarily enroll them in religiously affiliated non-public schools; and, whether there are specific safeguards that public school administrators must put in place pursuant to the delivery of special education services to children in religious schools.

CHILDREN ENROLLED IN RELIGIOUSLY AFFILIATED NON-PUBLIC SCHOOLS

As noted earlier, the IDEA does not direct boards of education to serve all children in religiously affiliated non-public schools. Rather, the IDEA requires boards to spend a proportionate share of their federal funds on students who are enrolled in non-public schools.[101] As long as boards spend the minimum amount of federal funds on these pupils, they will have met their obligations under the IDEA, even if all eligible children are not served. Accordingly, it is conceivable that school boards could serve some, but not all of these students. By way of illustration, boards could choose to serve only students with mild to moderate disabilities in the more common categories but not those with low-incidence disabilities.

Under the IDEA's provisions, local school boards can spend all of the money available pursuant to their proportionate share of federal funds on a select group of children in non-public schools and none on the rest of the students. Alternatively, boards may provide services to all students with disabilities who attend non-public schools but each would receive only a proportionate share of services. In the latter instance, the share of services that children in non-public schools would receive is likely to be much less than what their similarly situated peers would receive in public schools.[102] At the same time, the IDEA continues to require boards to locate and identify students with disabilities who are attending non-public schools.[103]

DELIVERY OF SERVICES

The IDEA's regulations grant public school officials a great deal of latitude over where and how special education services are offered to children in non-public schools.[104] Although the 1997 IDEA Amendments incorporated *Agostini v. Felton*'s holding that allows public school boards to provide the on-site delivery of certain federally funded services at religiously affiliated non-public schools, the Act does not mandate such delivery. The latitude that educators have over the delivery of services presumably includes the location where they are offered. Before acting, though, public school officials must consult with representatives from the non-public schools and give them the opportunity to express their views.[105]

Case law supports the notion that school boards have satisfied the IDEA once they offer a student with a disability a FAPE. Consequently, if parents reject the delivery of services offered at public schools, boards are under no legal obligation to make them available in non-public schools. The fact that an individual right to services does not exist can be found in the regulation which declares that the due process provisions of the IDEA are unavailable to students in non-public schools other than those relating to child find.[106] The Tenth Circuit's analysis in *Fowler* also indicated that school board officials merely had to make a proportionate share of their federal funds available to students in non-public schools.

In choosing where and how special education services are provided to children in non-public schools, administrators must make sure that they do not discriminate against a particular class of non-public school students. In other words, as in the case from Minnesota discussed earlier,[107] educators cannot refuse to provide on-site services to children in religiously affiliated non-public schools while offering them to peers in nonsectarian institutions.

If school systems do not offer the on-site delivery of services and children from religiously affiliated non-public schools must travel to other locations, boards may be required to provide transportation. Insofar as transportation is a related service under the IDEA, boards must provide it where it is necessary for students to benefit from special education.[108] School boards may also have to offer transportation between sites when students need it in order to access related services. Courts have held that transportation is necessary if students require it but can be dispensed with if they can safely access services without transportation.

SERVICES AVAILABLE

Pursuant to the IDEA and its regulations, students who attend non-public schools do not have the right to the same level of services that they would have received had they been in public schools. Consistent with decisions from both the Fifth and Seventh Circuits,[109] since individual students lack the right to receive any services at all, boards are under no obligation to provide any particular level of services.

School boards that offer services to students in non-public schools need not spend more on them than on children in public schools for similar services. In fact, students in non-public schools can receive lesser services than similarly situated peers in public schools if the cost of delivery to the former is greater than the cost of delivering the same to the latter.[110] The regulations support this interpretation in stating that individual students in non-public schools do not have the right to the same level of services that they would have received in public schools.[111]

At the same time, both the IDEA and the regulations indicate that boards may pay for services for students in non-public schools only up to an amount equal to the federal funds that they would have spent on them if they were enrolled in public schools.[112] As such, if boards offer services to students with disabilities in non-public schools, they may provide only a level of services to each student that can be paid for with the proportionate share of federal funds. The net result is that in such a situation each student would be likely to receive a bare minimum of services.

The regulations dictate that boards providing services to individual students must employ personnel who meet the same certification standards as their counterparts in the public schools.[113] The regulations add that students in non-public schools do not have the right to receive the same amount of services as their peers in the public schools.[114] Consequently, while public school officials have some discretion in limiting the kind and extent of the services that they offer to children who attend religiously affiliated non-public schools, once they commit to provide services, they must be of comparable quality.

SAFEGUARDS FOR THE ON-SITE DELIVERY OF SERVICES

The Supreme Court, in *Aguilar v. Felton*,[115] decided that the New York City Board of Education (NYCBOE) violated the Establishment Clause by allowing teachers and counselors paid with Title I funds to enter religiously affiliated non-public schools, mostly Roman Catholic schools and Hebrew day academies, to provide services to students. The Court struck down the practice even though the NYCBOE had controls in place based on its unfounded fear of excessive entanglement between educators in the public and the religiously affiliated non-public schools.

Twelve years later, in *Agostini v. Felton* (*Agostini*),[116] the Supreme Court took the extraordinary step of expressly repudiating *Aguilar* by dissolving the injunction that enforced its earlier judgment. In *Agostini* the Court found that the NYCBOE, and, by extension, other school boards, could, if they wished, but were not required to, provide Title I services on-site in religious schools. Relying in large part on the fact that the NYCBOE spent over $100 million on computer-aided instruction, leasing sites and mobile instructional units, and transporting students to those locations since 1986, the Court agreed that since appropriate procedures were in place, the funds would have been better spent educating students.[117]

The guidelines that the NYCBOE adopted in *Agostini* are relevant to special educators for two important reasons. First, since both the IDEA and Title I are federal laws, they are likely to be interpreted in a similar fashion. Second, the last of twenty-five questions in a memorandum issued by the Secretary of Education Richard W. Riley and the Department of Education shortly after *Agostini* was resolved indicated that it applies to federal programs other than Title I. According to the Department of Education:

> Question 25: Does the Supreme Court's decision in *Agostini* apply to other Federal education programs?
>
> Answer: The Supreme Court's decision dealt directly with the issue of the constitutionality of providing instructional services under Title I, Part A programs in private schools. However, the implication of the Court's ruling is that there is no constitutional bar to public school employees providing educational services in private schools under other Federal programs under similar circumstances.[118]

To the extent that many, but not all, of the safeguards that the NYCBOE used are incorporated in the memorandum from the Department of Education, it should be instructive in developing programs providing the on-site delivery of special education to students who attend religiously affiliated non-public schools.

The NYCBOE instituted safeguards for its personnel who worked in religious schools under Title I. First, only staff members who volunteered to do so were eligible to serve as Title I personnel in religiously affiliated non-public schools. Second, assignments were made without regard to the religious affiliations of the public employees, most of whom worked in schools that were not affiliated with their own religious beliefs. Third, Title I staff members were supervised by field personnel from the NYCBOE who made frequent unannounced visits on at least a monthly basis. Fourth, all religious symbols were removed from the classrooms and offices used in Title I programs. Fifth, as itinerants, most Title I staff ordinarily did not spend a full week in one location. Sixth, the Title I personnel were told to limit their discussions with classroom teachers and other staff in the religious schools to matters of mutual concern over the education of the Title I students.

Title I personnel were also given detailed instructions highlighting the secular nature and purpose of that law while explaining the importance of avoiding excessive entanglement. First, staff members were reminded that, as public school employees, they were responsible only to their own supervisors. Second, public employees were told that they could instruct only students who were approved by their supervisors. Third, staff members were warned not to engage in team teaching or other cooperative instructional methodologies with personnel from the religious schools. Fourth, public employees were forbidden from introducing any religious materials in their classrooms and work areas. Fifth, staff members were told to avoid involvement in religious activities at the schools where they worked. Finally, public employees were reminded that all materials and equipment purchased with Title I funds were to be used solely in that program.

Clearly, these guidelines provide a way to maintain a healthy separation between religiously affiliated non-public schools. Unfortunately, in light of the changes in the IDEA and its regulations, even these safeguards may be for naught if public school officials stick to the letter of the law and do not expand the range of services available to children who attend non-public schools.

STATE LAWS

It is important to recognize that state constitutions, laws, and regulations may provide additional requirements and restrictions regarding the provision of special education services to students attending nonpublic schools.[119] First, although the Supreme Court has held that the Establishment Clause does not prohibit the on-site delivery of educational services at sectarian schools,[120] state constitutions, under so-called Blaine Amendments, may be more restrictive.

The Blaine Amendment was a failed constitutional amendment that Senator James K. Blaine of Maine introduced in 1875 in an attempt to prevent aid from going to schools "under the control of any religious sect,"[121] language that, at that time, was applied to the Roman Catholic Church and its schools. Although the Amendment was defeated in 1876, thirty-six states, plus the Commonwealth of Puerto Rico, include Blaine-type language in their constitutions that impose significant limits on the relationship between religious institutions and state governments.[122] Moreover, state special education statutes and their regulations may require public school boards to provide more to students with disabilities voluntarily attending private schools than is mandated by the IDEA.

As noted earlier, the IDEA[123] and its regulations[124] authorize the federal Secretary of Education to provide special education services directly through a by-pass procedure when the provision of such services violates more restrictive state constitutions. The maximum amount of money available per student for when the Secretary engages in a by-pass is determined by dividing the total amount received by a state under the IDEA for the fiscal year by the number of children with disabilities served in the prior year as reported to the Department of Education by the number of private school children with disabilities in the state.[125]

In a case from Missouri that was cited earlier, the Eighth Circuit upheld the state's refusal to allow public school educators to provide on-site services at a religious school under the state's constitution. However, the court suggested in dicta that the by-pass provision was an available remedy whenever a state law frustrates the provision of services under the IDEA.[126]

While the provision of on-site services in private schools is permitted but not mandated by the IDEA, it can be required under state statutes and regulations. For example, a federal trial court in New York initially ruled that although the IDEA did not compel a local school board to provide a one-on-one aide to a student who attended a religious school, it was required to do so at his school under state law.[127] However, on appeal, the Second Circuit vacated the trial court's judgment and dismissed the case on the basis that it lacked jurisdiction over New York's incorporation of the IDEA into state law.[128] In other words, the court concluded that since the dispute did not involve a question of federal law, the case should not have been in federal court. Even so, a state court in New York relied on the same law in ordering a public school board to provide on-site nursing services to a student with diabetes in her religiously affiliated non-public school.[129] In its analysis, the court referenced another state law mandating that all students in non-public schools were to be provided with the same health, welfare services, and facilities as were available to children who attended public schools.[130]

In another example, an appellate court in Pennsylvania, relying partially on commonwealth law, ruled that a school board could not condition the receipt of related services on having a student from a religiously affiliated non-public school enroll in a public school. The student received speech and language services from an intermediate unit while he attended a religious school. When the intermediate unit ceased providing services, the student's parents asked the local board to offer the aid. The local board developed an IEP for the child but conditioned the receipt of services on his enrolling in a public school.

On further review of an administrative order in favor of the board, an appellate court reversed in favor of the parents.[131] Conceding that the board was not required to provide the services on-site at the religious school, the court ruled that pursuant to a commonwealth statute, students in non-public schools had an equal opportunity to participate in public school programs.[132] The court refused to interpret the IDEA as supporting a denial of services that would have been provided at a public school facility for students enrolled in public schools, particularly where allowing the student from the religious school to participate in the classes would not have caused the board an additional expenditure of funds.

NOTES

1. *Everson v. Board of Educ.*, 330 U.S. 1 (1947), *reh'g denied*, 330 U.S. 855 (1947).

2. Previously, in *Cochran v. Louisiana State Board of Education*, 281 U.S. 370 (1930), the Supreme Court affirmed the constitutionality of a statute that provided textbooks for students regardless of whether they attended religious schools. However, the Court decided this case under the Due Process Clause of the Fourteenth Amendment rather than the First Amendment.

3. The Supreme Court expanded the boundaries of the child benefit test in *Board of Educ. v. Allen*, 392 U.S. 236 (1968) wherein it upheld a statute from New York that required local school boards to loan textbooks for secular instruction to all children in grades seven to twelve regardless of where they attended school.

4. For a review of the major cases involving government aid to religiously affiliated non-public schools, *see* Charles J. Russo, Gerald M. Cattaro, and Allan G. Osborne Jr., "State Aid to Religiously Affiliated Non-Public Schools: An Emerging Trend or Same Old Same Old?" 8 *Journal of Research in Christian Education*, No. 2, 267 (1999).

5. 403 U.S. 602 (1971).

6. 403 U.S. at 612–613 (internal citations omitted). When addressing entanglement and state aid to institutions that are religiously affiliated, Chief Justice Warren Burger noted that the Court took three additional factors into consideration: "[w]e must examine the character and purposes of the institutions that are benefitted, the nature of the aid that the State provides, and the resulting relationship between the government and religious authority." *Lemon v. Kurtzman*, 403 U.S. 602, 615 (1971).

7. 473 U.S. 402 (1985).

8. Title I of the Elementary and Secondary Education Act, 20 U.S.C.A. §§ 2701 *et seq.*

9. As a result of *Aguilar*, one researcher estimated that 30 percent of all eligible Title I students in religiously affiliated non-public schools were deprived of educational benefits that they were entitled to receive under Title I. *See* Ralph D. Mawdsley and Charles J. Russo, "Supreme Court Upholds Religious Liberty: Educational Implications," 84 *Education Law Reporter*, 877, 893 n. 141 (1993).

10. The metamorphosis actually began in *Witters v. Washington Department of Servs. for the Blind*, 474 U.S. 481 (1986) (holding that the First Amendment did not preclude a state from extending aid under a vocational rehabilitation assistance program to a blind student who chose to study at a Christian college to become a pastor, missionary, or youth director on the basis that the help was generally available without regard for the sectarian or nonsectarian nature of the institution), *rehearing denied, Witters v. Washington Dep't of Servs. for the Blind*, 475 U.S. 1091 (1986). The Supreme Court of Washington, in *Witters v. State Comm'n for the Blind*, 771 P.2d 1119 (Wash. 1989), *cert. denied sub nom. Witters v. Washington Dept. of Servs. for the Blind*, 493 U.S. 850 (1989) subsequently found that language in the state constitution prohibited the use of public funds for religious instruction.

11. 509 U.S. 1 (1993).

12. For a comprehensive discussion of this case *see* Allan G. Osborne, "Providing Special Education and Related Services to Parochial School Students in the Wake of *Zobrest*," 87 *Education Law Reporter* 329 (1994).

13. 521 U.S. 203 (1997).

14. For more detailed information on this decision *see* Allan G. Osborne and Charles J. Russo, "The Ghoul Is Dead, Long Live the Ghoul: *Agostini v. Felton* and the Delivery of Title I Services in Non-Public Schools," 119 *Education Law Reporter* 781 (1997).

15. *Helms v. Cody*, 856 F. Supp. 1102 (E.D. La. 1994), *aff'd in part, rev'd in part sub nom. Helms v. Picard*, 151 F.3d 347 (5th Cir. 1998), *cert. granted sub nom. Mitchell v. Helms*, 527 U.S. 1114 (1999), *rev'd* 527 U.S. 1002 (2000), *on remand*, 229 F.3d 467 (5th Cir. 2000).

16. For a discussion of this case and its implications, see Ralph D. Mawdsley and Charles J. Russo, "Religious Schools and Government Assistance: What Is Acceptable After Helms?" 151 *Education Law Reporter* 373 (2001).

17. Chapter 2 of Title I [now Title VI] of the Elementary and Secondary Education Act, 20 U.S.C.A.§§ 7301-7373.

18. In the part of the case most relevant to special education, the Fifth Circuit, in *Helms v. Picard*, 151 F.3d 347 (5th Cir. 1998), reversed an earlier trial court judgment and upheld a state law that permitted the on-site delivery of special education services to children who attended Catholic schools; the court also affirmed the constitutionality of a state law that provided that these same children were entitled to free transportation to and from school. These parts of the case were not appealed to the Supreme Court.

19. 536 U.S. 639 (2002).

20. For a discussion of this case and its implications, *see* Charles J. Russo and Ralph D. Mawdsley, "Vouchers before the Supreme Court: Predictions and Implications," 163 *Education Law Reporter* 555 (2002).

21. For a discussion of these issues under the 1999 regulations, *see* Charles J. Russo, Joseph D. Massucci, and Allan G. Osborne Jr., "The Delivery of Special Education Services in Catholic Schools: One Hand Gives, the Other Hand Takes Away," *Catholic Education: A Journal of Inquiry and Practice*, vol. 3, no. 3, 375 (2000).

22. *See* Christina A. Samuels, "Private Schools Hail Changes to IDEA," *Education Week*, May 18, 2005, pp. 1, 24.

23. 20 U.S.C.A. § 1412(a)(10).

24. 34 C.F.R. § 300.132.

25. 20 U.S.C.A. § 1412(a)(10)(A)(i)(III).

26. *See Meek v. Pittenger*, 421 U.S. 349 (1975), *Wolman v. Walter*, 433 U.S. 229 (1977).

27. 34 C.F.R. § 76.1 *et seq.*

28. 34 C.F.R. § 76.651(a)(1).

29. 34 C.F.R. § 76.654(a).

30. 34 C.F.R. §§ 76.652(a)(1)–(5).

31. 34 C.F.R. § 300.131(a).

32. 34 C.F.R. § 300.132.

33. 34 C.F.R. § 300.130.
34. 34 C.F.R. § 300.133.
35. 20 U.S.C.A. §§ 1412(a)(10)(A)(i)(I),(II).
36. 20 U.S.C.A. § 1412(a)(10)(A)((i)(iv); 34 C.F.R. § 300.133(d).
37. 34 C.F.R. § 300.141.
38. 34 C.F.R. § 300.143.
39. 34 C.F.R. § 300.142(a).
40. 34 C.F.R. § 300.142(b).
41. 34 C.F.R. § 300.144(c).
42. 34 C.F.R. § 300.137(a). For a case reiterating this principle, see *Foley v. Special School Dist. of St. Louis County*, 153 F.3d 863 (8th Cir. 1998).
43. The regulations addressing comparable services are derived on 20 U.S.C.A. § 1412(a)(10).
44. 34 C.F.R. § 300.137(b)(2).
45. 1412(a)(10)(A)(iii)(I).
46. 34 C.F.R. § 300.137(c)(2).
47. 1412(a)(10)(A)(iv).
48. 20 U.S.C.A. § 1412(a)(10)(v)(I).
49. 34 C.F.R. § 300.138(a)(1).
50. For a case affirming the provision of lesser benefits under the IDEA to a student who attended a religious school, *see Gary S. v. Manchester School District*, 374 F.3d 15 (1st Cir. 2004), *cert. denied*, 543 U.S. 988 (2004).
51. 34 C.F.R. § 300.138(a)(2).
52. 34 C.F.R. § 300.138(b)(1).
53. 34 C.F.R. § 300.138(b)(2).
54. 20 U.S.C.A. § 1412(a)(10)(vi)(II).
55. 34 C.F.R. § 300.139(a).
56. 20 U.S.C.A. § 1412(a)(10)(vi)(I).
57. 34 C.F.R. § 300.139(a).
58. 34 C.F.R. § 300.139(b)(1)(i)(A).
59. 34 C.F.R. § 300.139(b)(1)(i)(B).
60. 34 C.F.R. § 300.139(b)(1)(B)(ii).
61. 34 C.F.R. § 300.139(b)(2).
62. 34 C.F.R. § 300.140(a).
63. 34 C.F.R. § 300.140(b).
64. 34 C.F.R. § 300.140(c).
65. 20 U.S.C.A. § 1412(f)(1). *See also* 34 C.F.R. §§ 300.190-198.
66. 20 U.S.C.A. § 1412(f)(2).
67. 20 U.S.C.A. § 1412(f)(3).
68. 20 U.S.C.A. § 1412(a)(10)(A)(I); 34 C.F.R. § 300.131(a).
69. 34 C.F.R. § 300.131(b)(2).
70. 34 C.F.R. § 300.131(c).
71. 34 C.F.R. § 300.131(d).

72. *Goodall v. Stafford County School Bd.*, 930 F.2d 363 (4th Cir. 1991).

73. *Zobrest v. Catalina Foothills School Dist.*, 509 U.S. 1 (1993).

74. *Goodall v. Stafford County School Bd.*, 60 F.3d 168 (4th Cir. 1995).

75. *Tribble v. Montgomery*, 798 F. Supp. 668 (M.D. Ala. 1992); *Foley v. Special School Dist. of St. Louis County*, 927 F. Supp. 1214 (E.D. Mo. 1996); *motion for reconsideration denied* 968 F. Supp. 481 (E.D. Mo. 1997), *aff'd,*153 F.3d 863 (8th Cir. 1998); *K.R. v. Anderson Community School Corp.*, 81 F.3d 673 (7th Cir. 1996), *vacated and remanded,* 521 U.S. 1114 (1997) (mem.), *on remand,* 125 F.3d 1017 (7th Cir. 1997), *cert. denied,* 523 U.S. 1046 (1998); *Cefalu v. East Baton Rouge Parish School Bd.*, 117 F.3d 231 (5th Cir. 1997); previous decision at 103 F.3d 393 (5th Cir. 1997) withdrawn.

76. *Natchez-Adams School District v. Searing,* 918 F. Supp. 1028 (S.D. Miss. 1996).

77. *K.R. v. Anderson Community School Corp.*, 81 F.3d 673 (7th Cir. 1996), *vacated and remanded,* 521 U.S. 1114 (1997) (mem.), *on remand* 125 F.3d 1017 (7th Cir. 1997); *Russman v. Sobol,* 85 F.3d 1050 (2d Cir. 1996), *vacated and remanded,* 521 U.S. 1114 (1997) (mem.), *reversed and remanded on remand sub nom. Russman v. Mills,* 150 F.3d 219 (2d Cir. 1998); *Fowler v. Unified School Dist.*, 107 F.3d 797 (10th Cir. 1997a), *vacated and remanded,* 521 U.S. 1115 (1997) (mem.), *on remand,* 129 F.3d 1431 (10th Cir. 1997).

78. *See Roslyn Union Free School Dist. v. University of the State of N.Y., State Educ. Dep't,* 711 N.Y.S.2d 582 (N.Y. App. Div. 2000) (affirming that a school board was not required to provide a child with transportation to a private after-school program on the basis that it had not denied the student access to its after-school program).

79. 34 C.F.R. § 300.34, 319(b)(1)(ii).

80. *Felter v. Cape Girardeau School Dist.*, 810 F. Supp. 1062 (E.D. Mo. 1993).

81. *Donald B. v. Board of School Commissioners of Mobile County,* 117 F.3d 1371 (11th Cir. 1997).

82. *K .R. v. Anderson Community School Corp.*, 521 U.S. 1114 (1997) (mem.), *on remand* 125 F.3d 1017 (7th Cir. 1997), *cert. denied,* 523 U.S. 1046 (1998); *Russman v. Sobol, vacated and remanded,* 521 U.S. 1114 (1997) (mem.), *reversed and remanded on remand sub nom. Russman v. Mills,* 150 F.3d 219 (2d Cir. 1998); *Fowler v. Unified School Dist., vacated and remanded,* 521 U.S. 1115 (1997) (mem.), *on remand,* 129 F.3d 1431 (10th Cir. 1997).

83. *K.R. v. Anderson Community School Corp.*, 81 F.3d 673 (7th Cir. 1996), *vacated and remanded,* 521 U.S. 1114 (1997) (mem.).

84. *K.R. v. Anderson Community School Corp.*, 125 F.3d 1017 (7th Cir. 1997).

85. *Nieuwenhuis v. Delavan-Darien School Dist. Bd. of Educ.*, 996 F. Supp. 855 (E.D. Wis. 1998).

86. *Fowler v. Unified School Dist.*, 107 F.3d 797 (10th Cir. 1997).

87. *Fowler v. Unified School Dist.*, 129 F.3d 1431 (10th Cir. 1997).

88. *Russman v. Sobol,* 85 F.3d 1050 (2d Cir. 1996), *vacated and remanded,* 521 U.S. 1114 (1997) (mem.).

89. *Russman v. Mills,* 150 F.3d 219 (2d Cir. 1998). The name of the case changed when New York State named a new Commissioner of Education.

90. *Russman v. Board of Educ. of the Enlarged City School Dist. of the City of Watervliet*, 92 F. Supp.2d 93 (N.D.N.Y. 2000).

91. *Cefalu v. East Baton Rouge Parish School Bd.*, 103 F.3d 393 (5th Cir. 1997) *withdrawn.*

92. *Cefalu v. East Baton Rouge Parish School Bd.*, 117 F.3d 231 (5th Cir. 1997), *previous decision at* 103 F.3d 393 (5th Cir. 1997) *withdrawn.*

93. *Foley v. Special School Dist. of St. Louis County*, 927 F. Supp. 1214 (E.D. Mo. 1996); *motion for reconsideration denied* 968 F. Supp. 481 (E.D. Mo. 1997), *aff'd* 153 F.3d 863 (8th Cir. 1998).

94. *Peter v. Wedl*, 155 F.3d 992 (8th Cir. 1998), *on remand sub. nom Westendorp v. Independent School Dist. No. 273*, 35 F. Supp. 2d (Minn. 1998).

95. *Westendorp v. Independent School Dist. No. 273*, 35 F. Supp. 2d 1134 (D. Minn. 1998).

96. *Bristol Warren Reg. School Comm. v. Rhode Island Dep't of Elementary and Secondary Educ.*, 253 F. Supp.2d 236 (D.R.I. 2003).

97. *Gabel ex rel. L.G. v. Board of Educ. of the Hyde Park Cent. School Dist.*, 368 F. Supp.2d 313 (S.D.N.Y. 2005).

98. *Board of Educ. of the Appoquinimink School District v. Johnson*, 543 F. Supp.2d 351 (D. Del. 2008).

99. *Jasa v. Millard Pub. School Dist. No. 17*, 206 F.3d 813 (8th Cir. 2000).

100. *Gary S. v. Manchester School Dist.*, 241 F. Supp.2d 111 (D.N.H. 2003), aff'd, 374 F.3d 15 (1st Cir. 2004).

101. 20 U.S.C.A. § 1412(a)(10)(A)(i)(I).

102. 34 C.F.R. §§ 300.137–138.

103. 34 C.F.R. § 300.131.

104. *But see Board of Educ. of Kiryas Joel Village School Dist. v. Grument*, 512 U.S. 687 (1994) (striking down the creation of a public school district to serve the needs of children with disabilities where its boundaries were identical to those of their religious community).

105. 34 C.F.R.§ 300.134.

106. 34 C.F.R.§ 300.140.

107. *See* notes 94–95 and accompanying text.

108. 34 C.F.R. § 300.139.

109. *See*, in particular, notes 83 and 91–92 along with accompanying text.

110. 34 C.F.R. §§ 300.137, 138(a)(2).

111. 34 C.F.R. §§ 300.137, 138(a)(2).

112. 34 C.F.R. §§ 300.137, 138(a)(2).

113. 34 C.F.R. § 300.138(a)(1).

114. 34 C.F.R. § 300.138(a)(2).

115. 473 U.S. 402 (1985).

116. 521 U.S. 203 (1997).

117. *See* Charles J. Russo and Allan G. Osborne Jr., "*Agostini v. Felton*: Is the Demise of the Ghoul at Hand," 116 *Education Law Reporter* 515 (1997); Allan G. Osborne

Jr. and Charles J. Russo, "The Ghoul Is Dead, Long Live the Ghoul: *Agostini v. Felton* and the Delivery of Title I Services in Non-Public Schools," 119 *Education Law Reporter* 781 (1997).

118. United States Department of Education (1997, July). Guidance on the Supreme Court's Decision in *Agostini v. Felton* and Title I (Part A) of the Elementary and Secondary Education Act. www.ed.gov.legislation/ESEA/feltguid.html.

119. Ralph D. Mawdsley and Allan G. Osborne Jr., "Providing Special Education Services to Students in Religious Schools," 219 *Education Law Reporter* 347 (2007).

120. *Zobrest v. Catalina Foothills School District*, 509 U.S. 1(1993); *Agostini v. Felton*, 521 U.S. 203 (1997).

121. The proposed Amendment read:

> No State shall make any law respecting an establishment of religion or prohibiting the free exercise thereof; and no money raised by taxation in any State for the support of public schools, or derived from any public fund therefore, nor any public lands devoted thereto, shall ever be under the control of any religious sect, nor shall any money so raised or lands so devoted be divided between religious sects or denominations.

See 4 *Congressional Record* 205 (1875) (Blaine's statement submitting a proposed constitutional amendment to Congress).

122. For a discussion of the Blaine Amendment, *see Mitchell v. Helms*, 530 U.S. 793, 828–29 (2000), *reh'g denied*, 530 U.S. 1296 (2000), *on remand sub nom. Helms v. Picard*, 229 F.3d 467 (5th Cir. 2000).

123. 20 U.S.C.A. § 1412(f)(1).

124. 34 C.F.R. §§ 300.190–198.

125. 34 C.F.R. § 300.191.

126. *Foley v. Special School Dist. of St. Louis County*, 153 F.3d 863 (8th Cir. 1998).

127. *Bay Shore Union Free School Dist. v. T.*, 405 F. Supp.2d 230 (E.D.N.Y. 2005) *citing N.Y. Education Law* § 3602-c(3) .

128. *Bay Shore Union Free School Dist. v. T.*, 485 F.3d 739 (2d Cir. 2007).

129. *Richard K. v. Petrone*, 815 N.Y.S.2d 270 (N.Y. App. Div. 2006).

130. N.Y. EDUC. LAW § 912.

131. *Veschi v. Northwestern Lehigh School Dist.*, 772 A.2d 469 (Pa. Commw. Ct. 2001).

132. 22 Pa. Code § 14.41(e).

6

RECOMMENDATIONS FOR ADMINISTRATORS IN NON-PUBLIC SCHOOLS

This final chapter offers advice for parents and educational leaders in non-public schools who have, or are considering, special education programs.

GENERAL GUIDELINES

In working with all stakeholders to provide special education services for children whose parents would like them to attend religiously affiliated and other types of non-public schools, educators in both non-public and public schools should keep the lines of communication open by:

1. Working with Parents

Administrators and teachers in non-public schools who suspect that children have disabilities should notify parents of their concerns immediately; this can be done through telephone calls and with follow-up notes that can also serve as documentation. In fact, educational leaders in non-public schools should develop policies for the referral and assessment of students who are suspected as having disabilities.

The IDEA permits public school personnel to make evaluations regarding whether children need assessments for special education and who will conduct evaluations if they are deemed necessary. Even so, educators in non-public schools should consult with parents in a timely manner over the proposed testing of their children. At the same time, if they so choose, parents may prefer to have evaluations completed privately at their own expense.

If parents choose to have their children evaluated independently, either as a first step, or if they challenge the assessment performed by public school personnel, they should keep in mind that this can be an expensive process. In addition, education leaders should strive to keep parents informed at all times while providing them with appropriate reading materials, including Web sites, and support groups from which they can gain additional information about how their children are to be identified, assessed, and served.

2. Working with Public School Officials

If thorough assessments reveal that students have disabilities, administrators in non-public schools should contact officials in public schools to determine what services, if any, the home school boards of children are willing, and able, to provide. As noted earlier, while public school boards are required to spend a proportionate share of their federal funds on students with disabilities who attend non-public schools, they are not obligated to provide all of the required services that children may need.

Decisions about who is to be served and what services are to be provided are to be made by officials from the public schools in consultation with educational leaders from non-public schools. Moreover, it should be kept in mind that public school officials will have met their legal obligations to students in non-public schools once they committed a proportionate share of their federal funds to the education of these children.

Insofar as public schools often lack sufficient funds to provide all of the necessary services adequately for their own students, particularly at a time when resources for education are strained, most will be unable to do more than meet their legal obligations to students in non-public schools. Aware of this reality, administrators in non-public schools may need to understand that officials in public schools are not trying to be difficult. Rather, officials in public schools simply have fiscal constraints that place limits on their resources and are obligated to serve their children in their charge before they help other students.

3. Understanding the Parents' Dilemma

Parents may be required to balance their desire for a religion-based education with their child's need for special education services. Selecting which school their children are to attend can be a very difficult choice for parents. Administrators in non-public schools should understand these competing needs and work with parents to make decisions that are best for the children. In this regard, officials in non-public schools must make realistic assessments of what they can and will be able to provide for each child.

As discussed in the next point, frank discussions about what non-public schools may be able to offer should help parents to make the most appropriate decisions for their children. If parents eventually choose to place their children in public schools, officials in non-public schools must work with the parents and their colleagues in the public schools to help the student make a smooth transition.

4. Be Honest with Parents

Many parents expect that special education services will allow their children to "catch up" quickly with their peers. Unfortunately, since this is not often the case, educators in non-public schools need to discuss the possible outcomes of special education placements realistically with parents. In other words, educators should make it clear that in some situations, children may be able to remain in non-public schools and can develop many functional life skills but not earn high school diplomas. At the same time, educational leaders in non-public schools may have to bluntly prepare parents for the fact that since non-public schools cannot afford, either financially or in terms of staff, to serve their children, they may have to transfer to public schools in order to receive the most appropriate services for their children.

5. Being Prepared to Make Modifications

As illustrated above in the materials on Section 504 and the IDEA, many students with disabilities can succeed in regular classroom settings in non-public schools with modifications to learning environments and assignments. Thus, administrators in non-public schools should work with public school educators and evaluators as well as parents to design modifications that will allow students to be successful in their schools.

6. Providing Staff Development

Good teachers are able to meet the needs of most students with mild to moderate disabilities. Still, unfortunately, many good classroom teachers received little training in their own preparation programs for working with students with disabilities. Staff development programs can go a long way toward helping these teachers improve their skills so that they can better meet the needs of all students in their classrooms, not just a child or children with disabilities. Administrators in non-public schools should contact local public school officials to see what professional development activities are being offered to their own staffs, because most public schools are likely to be more than willing to allow teachers in non-public schools to attend these sessions since they are ultimately designed to assist children.

7. Examining Class Sizes

Although data are inconclusive, class sizes for students in special education classes need to be smaller than they were just a few years ago. Students in today's classrooms, in both public and non-public schools, have many needs that require a great deal of individualized attention. Even the best of teachers cannot meet the needs of all students in a large class. Smaller classes are much more conducive to educating students with mild to moderate disabilities within the regular education setting.

8. Understanding That Students with Disabilities Have the Same Rights to an Education as Their Peers Who Are Not Disabled

Consistent with religious teachings and principles of human rights generally, a major rule of the IDEA is that students with disabilities are, first and foremost, human beings with the same rights as all children, including the right to an appropriate education. This also means that all children have the same right to a religion-based education as other students if that is what their parents desire. To this end, educational leaders in religiously affiliated non-public schools should offer as much tutoring and other special education assistance as is feasible, both financially and in terms of staff resources, to allow students with disabilities to remain in their schools. While many parents must currently make a difficult decision between a religion-based education and needed special education services, perhaps some day they will not be required to make such a draconian choice.

SHARED ADVOCACY

The parents of many non-public students with disabilities are often surprised and distressed when they find out that the public schools will not provide their children with the same level of services they would receive if they were enrolled in the public schools. Understandably, these parents, as taxpayers, believe that having these services denied is unfair. Rather than belabor the point, administrators in non-public schools need to help parents understand that financially strapped public schools generally cannot do more than is required by law.

Instead of engaging in unproductive efforts to secure services for their children, the parents of students in non-public schools and the administrators of their schools should join with their public school counterparts to advocate for better funding for programs to serve all students with disabilities. For example, even more than three decades after the implementation of the original federal special education statute, Congress has still not come close to funding the IDEA's mandates fully. Increased federal funding for special education would result in more available funds to serve non-public school students with disabilities. All parents and educators need to join together to insist that Congress keeps its promises in this regard. With this in mind, we now turn to offer suggestions for educators and parents in non-public elementary and secondary schools.

RECOMMENDATIONS FOR ELEMENTARY SCHOOLS

Non-public schools, their students, parents, administrators, and teachers neither exist in isolation nor do the children enrolled in these institutions lose citizenship and educational rights "at the schoolhouse gate."[1] Yet, it is not reasonable to assume that non-public schools, especially those that are religiously affiliated, can meet the needs of all children with disabilities. As educational leaders in non-public schools embark on the path of inclusion, they must do all they can to learn about serving students with disabilities in non-public school environments. It is their professional ethical duty to validate the social and cultural capital that these students bring to their non-public school environments.

Consistent with the IDEA, opportunities in non-public schools should range from full-time placement in regular classes to self-contained classes to part-time programs with services provided in non-public and public schools. The needs of special education students can also be met by supplementary aids including pull-out programs using special education teachers, paraprofessionals, nontraditional technologies, peer partnerships, cross-age tutoring, and large-print books.

The new way of looking at how non-public schools meet the needs of all students, including those with disabilities, is a break from earlier prescriptions. Thus, from the outset, administrators in non-public elementary (and secondary) schools should seek to comply with the following IDEA checklist in order to assure that all students with disabilities:

- have access to the general education curriculum,
- receive special education that is a service, not a place to which they are sent,
- have options to receive a broad range of services addressing their needs,
- receive the assistance of an IEP team that first considers a placement in a local school with appropriate aids and services,
- can take advantage of a continuum of placement options,
- receive full access to procedural and substantive rights and that their parents are informed participants in the decision-making process,
- participate in programs that incorporate regular assessment strategies,

- have opportunities for involvement with nondisabled peers, and
- can use technological advancements that enable them to be educated in the least restrictive environment.

This new paradigm creates a paradox for the educators in non-public schools since it sets the tone for collaboration, inclusion, and doing the right thing for special needs children. Even so, educators in non-public schools must be careful not to raise the hopes of parents too high because providing a fully inclusive placement for some children may be an insurmountable challenge.

Placing a focus on the needs of children with disabilities means that administrators in private schools must provide leadership and support strategies in the shift from, in some instances, the nonexistence of special education programs to full inclusion. Such a shift in the implementation of services to students with special educational needs may well necessitate offering staff development, providing additional information for parents, and involving community advocates. The importance of institutional factors such as supportive faculty and staff, parents, and community members cannot be overlooked.

This stated, making such a change may be easier than it seems in non-public schools because of the limitations of the size of bureaucracy in implementing programs and not being constrained by preexisting or poor models.[2] Even though the IDEA challenges educators in non-public schools to seek new ways to support the needs of all students, they may have a prototype in Title I remedial programs in *Agostini v. Felton*. The challenge for educators in non-public schools is to set up strategic alliances, partnerships, and collaborative efforts with public school personnel and other agencies that help to develop a system-wide focus on improving teaching and learning, flexibility at the local level in tandem with clear accountability, clearly targeting resources, and stronger partnerships between schools and communities. The dynamics of political capital cannot be understated in the collaboration process between educational leaders in non-public and public schools.

The IDEA raises such key questions as which students will be identified and served, what services they will receive, and where they will be offered. In identifying which students are served, it is worth recalling that a public school board is only required to expend federal monies proportionate to the ratio of numbers of children with disabilities in non-public schools to the total number of such students in the district. It is also important to realize that many non-public schools provide services to students who live in different districts, an issue that can be important when dealing with the IDEA's child find provisions. As such, spending and the ratio of the numbers of students may vary from one district to the next, thereby confusing parents who seek equity for their children.

As administrators in non-public schools consult with parents, they would be wise to inform them that their children may have to forgo services that they might otherwise have received had they attended public schools. Moreover, administrators from non-public and public schools must consult over which services will be offered and/or which populations will be targeted. For example, this means that some dioceses may opt for speech pathology so that they may serve a broad group of students or may have to settle for services in grades kindergarten through sixth (K–6) in an effort to provide early needs assessments. In this way, it bears repeating that the amount of available benefits may vary depending on the relationships that educational leaders in non-public schools have established with their counterparts in local public schools.

It goes without saying that parents are a child's best advocate. Together, if there is a question whether a child needs special education, parents and non-public school administrators or school counselors (if available) should set up an appointment with public school officials to discuss whether the child can be assessed. If it turns out that a child needs special education, then his or her parents will have the opportunity to serve on the child's IEP team and help to shape the learning environment in which he or she will be educated. Depending on a child's needs, an IEP team should help school staff to identify the range, or continuum, of available services.

Students with disabilities should be placed in special classes, separate schools, or removed from a regular educational environment only when the nature or severity of a disability is such that, even with the use of supplementary aids and services, education cannot be satisfactorily achieved in an inclusive setting. Although it may be implausible to think that all students in non-public schools will benefit from all possible options under the IDEA, they have a greater likelihood of availing themselves of some of these programs by having necessary interventions and services and providing opportunities for involvement with nondisabled peers.

As to how and where services can be provided, once again the Title I model provides some guidance. Under Title I, services can be delivered on-site in non-public schools since they are for the child and not the school. Yet, even if an IEP team recommends that a child receive services in non-public schools, nothing permanent can be built there nor any of the equipment be utilized for religious instruction or anything to do with worship. The Title I model offers interesting options to explore when seeking programs for students in non-public schools. Among these choices are instructional services provided at a public school site, other public and privately owned neutral sites, or in mobile vans or portable units, educational radio or television, computer-assisted instruction, extended-day services, home tutoring, take-home computers, and interactive technology.

To the extent possible, the goal of IDEA is for students with disabilities to enroll at schools they would ordinarily have attended. The "neighborhood school" approach, which is predicated on students with disabilities being educated in their own communities, surrounded by siblings and friends, to the maximum extent possible, is beneficial to all children. Such an approach would be logical if all parents who choose non-public schools for their children could have special education services provided on-site. Until such time as states can provide special education services on-site in non-public schools, educational leaders in these schools must "render unto Caesar that which is Caesar's and to God that which is God's"[3] and do all that they can to provide an inclusive education for as many children with disabilities as is feasible.

In order to work toward full inclusion, educational leaders in non-public schools should involve all stakeholders in a planning process to create a new delivery model for students with disabilities since this should ensure the best use of resources to realize the potential of each child. The belief that non-public schools are the best place to encourage greater creativity and flexibility in the development of instructional designs for all children, including students with disabilities, seems to be the hope of parents who are depending on non-public schools to help educate their children.

RECOMMENDATIONS FOR HIGH SCHOOLS

Historically, religiously affiliated and other non-public high schools have worked hard to provide for individual differences among students despite lack of funding and programs similar to those available to children who attend public schools. True to the mission of the religious education, in particular, the dedication of the administrators, teachers, and other staff members along with the nurturing of local schools and their supporting churches, religious organizations, and/or communities have helped academically challenged students to experience success through classes geared to their ability and adjusted curricula. These efforts were evident long before students with disabilities became a focus of public concern and, ultimately, the law.

In discussing special education in non-public secondary schools, just as is the case with elementary schools, it is necessary to distinguish degrees of special education. All non-public schools, not just secondary schools, should be able to incorporate some or all of the following strategies to assist students with learning disabilities and moderate physical and behavioral disabilities by offering buildings and facilities that are readily accessible to the disabled; special tutoring programs staffed with appropriately trained/certified personnel; assessment procedures to determine the needs of individual students; classes geared to students with learning (and other) disabilities (content comparable with regular classes but employing teaching strategies designed to address special learning needs).

Specific accommodations, many of which require minimal expenditures, for students in need of special education should include individualized testing procedures such as additional time, oral testing, permitting tape-recording of class presentations, buddy system for note taking, outlines of class presentations for note taking (advance organizers), orientation programs for students to make them aware of their responsibilities to be of assistance to peers with special needs, and adapt/adjust co-curricular activities to students' physical abilities.

The number of students enrolled in non-public schools, other than those that have the mission of working exclusively with students with severe learning, physical, and behavioral disabilities is generally few. While it is beyond the scope of this book to attempt to determine why this is the case, it is the reality. In light of this reality, strategies employed to meet the needs of small numbers of students may differ dramatically from the strategies discussed herein. In seeking to provide better services for children with disabilities, educational leaders in non-public schools should consider not only exploring possible partnerships with local public schools but should also form collaborative efforts with other non-public high schools, even those of different faith communities in areas where several are close to one another. Collaborative efforts involving non-public schools might wish to consider one of the following forms:

1. Each school in an area could assume responsibility for providing a particular specialized service. Students with that need could enroll in that high school or enroll in their home high school and be transported for a portion of the day to avail themselves of that service.
2. One school in the area could service all the specialized needs and the other schools could contribute monetary and/or personnel resources to support the program.
3. On a regional basis, satellite schools strategically positioned in a geographical area could provide services for special needs students. These would be sponsored by a diocese, synod, state, or regional schools' association.
4. Cooperatively sponsored committees comprised of school representatives could be formed on a local level to determine student needs and available resources.
5. Provide ongoing staff development opportunities for all school personnel to address special education issues in religiously affiliated non-public schools in particular.
6. Local, state, or regional religious leaders might wish to pool some of their educational funds to provide resource specialists who focus on special education issues in non-public schools, communicate with local and state education agencies, and familiarize parents with the rights of children with disabilities.

7. School counselors and special education personnel should provide periodic individual and small group professional development sessions with faculty members. These sessions can be used to present strategies and techniques to be employed in classroom settings to address the special needs of students. These small group sessions should provide an atmosphere conducive to the exchange of professional ideas and continuous dialogue that could have a positive impact on teaching and learning. This approach should enable teachers to become involved in the identification process within the classroom contexts where student behaviors are exhibited.
8. School administrators could provide several opportunities in the beginning of the academic year for faculty members to visit schools with similar environments in order to observe firsthand programs that work well for special needs students. These teachers would in turn share their findings with colleagues in the home school, both in formal and informal settings, providing a support network among faculty.
9. Create a peer "study buddies" program in which student tutors are trained to provide assistance in core subject areas while receiving credit toward graduation community service requirements.

CONCLUSION

Recent statutory, regulatory, and judicial changes dealing with the delivery of special education in religiously affiliated non-public schools have left children in many religious schools with the proverbial half of a loaf of bread. That is, while the law makes it clear that students in religious schools are entitled to special education, the funding restrictions may actually limit the amount of services that they receive on-site. Thus, it is imperative to ensure that stakeholders in religiously affiliated and other non-public schools understand the parameters of the law of special education at both the federal and state levels so that they can work together to ensure that all children, including students with disabilities, receive the best possible education that they need—and deserve.

NOTES

1. *Tinker v. Des Moines Independent Community School District*, 393 U.S. 503, 505 (1969) (upholding the free speech rights of students) ("[i]t can hardly be argued that either students or teachers shed their constitutional rights to freedom of speech or expression at the schoolhouse gate.")

2. Gerald M. Cattaro, "Collaboration and Constructivism: A Case for the Nonpublic Schools" in *Curriculum Leadership: Rethinking Schools for the 21st Century*, Regis Bernhardt, Carolyn N. Hedley, Gerald M. Cattaro, and Vasilios Svolopoulos, eds., (Cresskill, NJ: Hampton Press, 1997), 69–88.

3. Luke 20:25.

APPENDIX A

SELECTED REGULATIONS, 34 C.F.R. §§ 300.118, 129-148

Sec. 300.118 Children in public or private institutions.

Except as provided in § 300.149(d) (regarding agency responsibility for general supervision for some individuals in adult prisons), an SEA must ensure that §300.114 is effectively implemented, including, if necessary, making arrangements with public and private institutions (such as a memorandum of agreement or special implementation procedures). (Authority: 20 U.S.C.A. § 1412(a)(5))

CHILDREN IN PRIVATE SCHOOLS

Sec. 300.129 State responsibility regarding children in private schools.

The State must have in effect policies and procedures that ensure that LEAs, and, if applicable, the SEA, meet the private school requirements in §§ 300.130 through 300.148. (Authority: 20 U.S.C.A. § 1412(a)(10))

Sec. 300.130 Definition of parentally-placed private school children with disabilities.

Parentally-placed private school children means children with disabilities enrolled by their parents in private, including religious, schools or facilities that meet the definition of elementary school in § 300.13 or secondary school in §300.36, other than children with disabilities covered under §§ 300.145 through 300.147. (Authority: 20 U.S.C.A. § 1412(a)(10)(A))

Sec. 300.131 Child find for parentally-placed private school children with disabilities.

(a) General. Each LEA must locate, identify, and evaluate all children with disabilities who are enrolled by their parents in private, including religious, elementary schools and secondary schools located in the school district served by the LEA, in accordance with paragraphs (b) through (e) of this section, and §§ 300.111 and 300.201.
(b) Child find design. The child find process must be designed to ensure—
  (1) The equitable participation of parentally-placed private school children; and
  (2) An accurate count of those children.
(c) Activities. In carrying out the requirements of this section, the LEA, or, if applicable, the SEA, must undertake activities similar to the activities undertaken for the agency's public school children.
(d) Cost. The cost of carrying out the child find requirements in this section, including individual evaluations, may not be considered in determining if an LEA has met its obligation under §300.133.
(e) Completion period. The child find process must be completed in a time period comparable to that for students attending public schools in the LEA consistent with §300.301.
(f) Out-of-State children. Each LEA in which private, including religious, elementary schools and secondary schools are located must, in carrying out the child find requirements in this section, include parentally-placed private school children who reside in a State other than the State in which the private schools that they attend are located. (Authority: 20 U.S.C.A. § 1412(a)(10)(A)(ii))

Sec. 300.132 Provision of services for parentally-placed private school children with disabilities—basic requirement.

(a) General. To the extent consistent with the number and location of children with disabilities who are enrolled by their parents in private, including religious, elementary schools and secondary schools located in the school district served by the LEA, provision is made for the participation of those children in the program assisted or carried out under Part B of the Act by providing them with special education and related services, including direct services determined in accordance with § 300.137, unless the Secretary has arranged for services to those children under the by-pass provisions in §§ 300.190 through 300.198.
(b) Services plan for parentally-placed private school children with disabilities. In accordance with paragraph (a) of this section and §§300.137 through 300.139, a services plan must be developed and implemented for each private school child with a disability who has been designated by the LEA in which the private school is located to receive special education and related services under this part.
(c) Record keeping. Each LEA must maintain in its records, and provide to the SEA, the following information related to parentally-placed private school children covered under §§300.130 through 300.144:

(1) The number of children evaluated;
(2) The number of children determined to be children with disabilities; and
(3) The number of children served. (Authority: 20 U.S.C.A. § 1412(a)(10)(A)(i))

Sec. 300.133 Expenditures.

(a) Formula. To meet the requirement of §300.132(a), each LEA must spend the following on providing special education and related services (including direct services) to parentally-placed private school children with disabilities:

(1) For children aged 3 through 21, an amount that is the same proportion of the LEA's total subgrant under section 1411(f) of

the Act as the number of private school children with disabilities aged 3 through 21 who are enrolled by their parents in private, including religious, elementary schools and secondary schools located in the school district served by the LEA, is to the total number of children with disabilities in its jurisdiction aged 3 through 21.

(2) (i) For children aged three through five, an amount that is the same proportion of the LEA's total subgrant under section 1419(g) of the Act as the number of parentally-placed private school children with disabilities aged three through five who are enrolled by their parents in a private, including religious, elementary school located in the school district served by the LEA, is to the total number of children with disabilities in its jurisdiction aged three through five.

(ii) As described in paragraph (a)(2)(i) of this section, children aged three through five are considered to be parentally-placed private school children with disabilities enrolled by their parents in private, including religious, elementary schools, if they are enrolled in private school that meets the definition of elementary school in § 300.13.

(3) If an LEA has not expended for equitable services all of the funds described in paragraphs (a)(1) and (a)(2) of this section by the end of the fiscal year for which Congress appropriated the funds, the LEA must obligate the remaining funds for special education and related services (including direct services) to parentally-placed private school children with disabilities during a carry-over period of one additional year.

(b) Calculating proportionate amount. In calculating the proportionate amount of Federal funds to be provided for parentally-placed private school children with disabilities, the LEA, after timely and meaningful consultation with representatives of private schools under § 300.134, must conduct a thorough and complete child find process to determine the number of parentally-placed children with disabilities attending private schools located in the LEA. (Appendix B for example of how to calculate proportionate share.)

(c) Annual count of the number of parentally-placed private school children with disabilities.

(1) Each LEA must—

(i) After timely and meaningful consultation with representatives of parentally-placed private school children with disabilities (consistent with §300.134), determine the number of parentally-placed private school children with disabilities attending private schools located in the LEA; and

(ii) Ensure that the count is conducted on any date between October 1 and December 1, inclusive, of each year.

(2) The count must be used to determine the amount that the LEA must spend on providing special education and related services to parentally-placed private school children with disabilities in the next subsequent fiscal year.

(d) Supplement, not supplant. State and local funds may supplement and in no case supplant the proportionate amount of Federal funds required to be expended for parentally-placed private school children with disabilities under this part. (Authority: 20 U.S.C.A. § 1412(a)(10)(A))

Sec. 300.134 Consultation.

To ensure timely and meaningful consultation, an LEA, or, if appropriate, an SEA, must consult with private school representatives and representatives of parents of parentally-placed private school children with disabilities during the design and development of special education and related services for the children regarding the following:

(a) Child find. The child find process, including—

(1) How parentally-placed private school children suspected of having a disability can participate equitably; and

(2) How parents, teachers, and private school officials will be informed of the process.

(b) Proportionate share of funds. The determination of the proportionate share of Federal funds available to serve parentally-placed private school children with disabilities under § 300.133(b), including the determination of how the proportionate share of those funds was calculated.

(c) Consultation process. The consultation process among the LEA, private school officials, and representatives of parents of parentally-placed private school children with disabilities, including how the process will operate throughout the school year to ensure that parentally-placed children with disabilities identified through the child find process can meaningfully participate in special education and related services.

(d) Provision of special education and related services. How, where, and by whom special education and related services will be provided for parentally-placed private school children with disabilities, including a discussion of—

(1) The types of services, including direct services and alternate service delivery mechanisms; and

(2) How special education and related services will be apportioned if funds are insufficient to serve all parentally-placed private school children; and

(3) How and when those decisions will be made;

(e) Written explanation by LEA regarding services. How, if the LEA disagrees with the views of the private school officials on the provision of services or types of services (whether provided directly or through a contract), the LEA will provide to the private school officials a written explanation of the reasons why the LEA chose not to provide services directly or through a contract. (Authority: 20 U.S.C.A. § 1412(a)(10)(A)(111))

Sec. 300.135 Written affirmation.

(a) When timely and meaningful consultation, as required by §300.134, has occurred, the LEA must obtain a written affirmation signed by the representatives of participating private schools.

(b) If the representatives do not provide the affirmation within a reasonable period of time, the LEA must forward the documentation of the consultation process to the SEA. (Authority: 20 U.S.C.A. § 1412(a)(10)(A)(iv))

Sec. 300.136 Compliance.

(a) General. A private school official has the right to submit a complaint to the SEA that the LEA—

(1) Did not engage in consultation that was meaningful and timely; or

(2) Did not give due consideration to the views of the private school official.

(b) Procedure.

(1) If the private school official wishes to submit a complaint, the official must provide to the SEA the basis of the noncompliance by the LEA with the applicable private school provisions in this part; and

(2) The LEA must forward the appropriate documentation to the SEA.

(3) (i) If the private school official is dissatisfied with the decision of the SEA, the official may submit a complaint to the Secretary by providing the information on noncompliance described in paragraph (b)(1) of this section; and

(ii) The SEA must forward the appropriate documentation to the Secretary. (Authority 20 U.S.C.A. § 1412(a)(10)(A)(v))

Sec. 300.137 Equitable services determined.

(a) No individual right to special education and related services. No parentally-placed private school child with a disability has an individual right to receive some or all special education and related services the child would receive if enrolled in a public school.

(b) Decisions.

(1) Decisions about the services that will be provided to parentally-placed private school children with disabilities under §§ 300.130 through 300.144 must be made in accordance with paragraph (c) of this section and § 300.134(C).

(2) The LEA must make the final decisions with respect to the services to be provided to eligible parentally-placed private school children with disabilities.

(c) Services plan for each child served under §§ 300.130 through 300.144. If a child with a disability is enrolled in a religious or other private school by the child's parents and will receive special education or related services from an LEA, the LEA must—

(1) Initiate and conduct meetings to develop, review, and revise a services plan for the child, in accordance with §300.138(b); and

(2) Ensure that a representative of the religious or other private school attends each meeting. If the representative cannot attend, the LEA shall use other methods to ensure participation by the religious or other private school, including individual or conference telephone calls. (Authority: 20 U.S.C.A. § 1412(a)(10)(A))

Sec. 300.138 Equitable services provided.

(a) General.

(1) The services provided to parentally-placed private school children with disabilities must be provided by personnel meeting the same standards as personnel providing services in the public schools, except that private elementary school and secondary school teachers who are providing equitable services to parentally-placed private school children with disabilities do not have to meet the highly qualified special education teacher requirements of §300.18.

(2) Parentally-placed private school children with disabilities may receive a different amount of services than children with disabilities in public schools.

(b) Services provided in accordance with a services plan.

(1) Each parentally-placed private school child with a disability who has been designated to receive services under § 300.132 must have a services plan that describes the specific special education and related services that the LEA will provide to the child in light of the services that the LEA has determined, through the process described in §§ 300.134 and 300.137, it will make available to parentally-placed private school children with disabilities.

(2) The services plan must, to the extent appropriate—

(i) Meet the requirements of § 300.320, or for a child ages three through five, meet the requirements of § 300.323(b) with respect to the services provided; and

(ii) Be developed, reviewed, and revised consistent with §§300.321 through 300.324.

(c) Provision of equitable services.

(1) The provision of services pursuant to this section and §§ 300.139 through 300.143 must be provided:

(i) By employees of a public agency; or

(ii) Through contract by the public agency with an individual, association, agency, organization, or other entity.

(2) Special education and related services provided to parentally-placed private school children with disabilities, including materials and equipment, must be secular, neutral, and nonideological. (Authority: 20 U.S.C.A. § 1412(a)(10)(A)(vi))

Sec. 300.139 Location of services and transportation.

(a) Services on private school premises. Services to parentally-placed private school children with disabilities may be provided on the premises of private, including religious, schools, to the extent consistent with law.

(b) Transportation.

(1) General.

(i) If necessary for the child to benefit from or participate in the services provided under this part, a parentally-placed private school child with a disability must be provided transportation—

(A) From the child's school or the child's home to a site other than the private school; and

(B) From the service site to the private school, or to the child's home, depending on the timing of the services.

(ii) LEAs are not required to provide transportation from the child's home to the private school.

(2) Cost of transportation. The cost of the transportation described in paragraph (b)(1)(i) of this section may be included in calculating whether the LEA has met the requirement of §300.133. (Authority: 20 U.S.C.A. § 1412(a)(10)(A)(3)

Sec. 300.140 Due process complaints and State complaints.

(a) Due process not applicable, except for child find. (1) Except as provided in paragraph (b) of this section, the procedures in §§ 300.504 through 300.519 do not apply to complaints that an LEA has failed to meet the requirements of §§300.132 through 300.139, including the provision of services indicated on the child's services plan.

(b) Child find complaints—to be filed with the LEA in which the private school is located.

(1) The procedures in §§ 300.504 through 300.519 apply to complaints that an LEA has failed to meet the child find requirements in §300.131, including the requirements in §§300.300 through 300.311.

(2) Any due process complaint regarding the child find requirements (as described in paragraph (b)(1) of this section) must be filed with the LEA in which the private school is located and a copy must be forwarded to the SEA.

(c) State complaints.

(1) Any complaint that an SEA or LEA has failed to meet the requirements in §§ 300.132 through 300.135 and 300.137 through 300.144 must be filed in accordance with the procedures described in §§300.151 through 300.153.

(2) Complaints filed by private school officials under §300.136(a) must be filed with SEA in accordance with §300.136(b). (Authority: 20 U.S.C.A. § 1412(a)(10)(A))

Sec. 300.141 Requirement that funds not benefit a private school.

(a) An LEA may not use funds provided under section 1411 or 1419 of the Act to finance the existing level of instruction in a private school or to otherwise benefit the private school.

(b) The LEA must use funds provided under Part B of the Act to meet the special education and related services needs of parentally-placed private school children with disabilities,
but not for meeting—

(1) The needs of a private school; or

(2) The general needs of the students enrolled in the private school. (Authority: 20 U.S.C.A. § 1412(a)(10)(A))

Sec. 300.142 Use of personnel.

(a) Use of public school personnel. An LEA may use funds available under sections 1411 and 1419 of the Act to make public school personnel available in other than public facilities—

(1) To extent necessary to provide services under §§300.130 through 300.144; and

(2) If those services are not normally provided by the private school.

(b) Use of private school personnel. An LEA may use funds available under sections 1411 and 1419 of the Act to pay for the services of an employee of a private school to provide services under §§ 300.130 through 300.144 if—

(1) The employee performs the services outside of his or her regular hours of duty; and

(2) The employee performs the services under public supervision and control. (Authority: 20 U.S.C.A. § 1412(a)(10)(A))

Sec. 300.143 Separate classes prohibited.

An LEA may not use funds available under section 1411 or 1419 of the Act for classes that are organized separately on the basis of school enrollment or religion of the children if—

(a) The classes are at the same site; and

(b) The classes include children enrolled in public schools and children enrolled in private schools. (Authority: 20 U.S.C.A. § 1412(a)(10)(A))

Sec. 300.144 Property, equipment, and supplies.

(a) A public agency must control and administer the funds used to provide special education and related services under §§ 300.137

through 300.139, and hold title to and administer materials, equipment, and property purchased with those funds for the uses and purposes provided in the Act.

(b) The public agency may place equipment and supplies in a private school for the period of time needed for the Part B program.

(c) The public agency must ensure that the equipment and supplies placed in a private school—

(1) Are used only for Part B purposes; and

(2) Can be removed from the private school without remodeling the private school facility.

(d) The public agency must remove equipment and supplies from a private school if—

(1) The equipment and supplies are no longer needed for Part B purposes; or

(2) Removal is necessary to avoid unauthorized use of the equipment and supplies for other than Part B purposes.

(e) No funds under Part B of the Act may be used for repairs, minor remodeling, or construction of private school facilities. (Authority: 20 U.S.C.A. § 1412(a)(10)(A)(vii))

CHILDREN WITH DISABILITIES IN PRIVATE SCHOOLS PLACED OR REFERRED BY PUBLIC AGENCIES

Sec. 300.145 Applicability of §§300.146 through 300.147.

Sections 300.146 through 300.147 apply only to children with disabilities who are or have been placed in or referred to a private school or facility by a public agency as a means of providing special education and related services. (Authority: 20 U.S.C.A. § 1412(a)(10)(B))

Sec. 300.146 Responsibility of SEA.

Each SEA must ensure that a child with a disability who is placed in or referred to a private school or facility by a public agency—

(a) Is provided special education and related services—

(1) In conformance with an IEP [individualized education program] that meets the requirements of §§ 300.320 through 300.325; and

(2) At no cost to the parents;

(b) Is provided an education that meets the standards that apply to education provided by the SEA and LEAs including the requirements of this part, except for §300.18 and §300.156(C); and

(c) Has all of the rights of a child with a disability who is served by a public agency. (Authority: 20 U.S.C.A. § 1412(a)(10)(B))

Sec. 300.147 Implementation by SEA.

In implementing § 300.146, the SEA must—

(a) Monitor compliance through procedures such as written reports, on-site visits, and parent questionnaires;

(b) Disseminate copies of applicable standards to each private school and facility to which a public agency has referred or placed a child with a disability; and

(c) Provide an opportunity for those private schools and facilities to participate in the development and revision of State standards that apply to them. (Authority: 20 U.S.C.A §. 1412(a)(10)(B))

CHILDREN WITH DISABILITIES ENROLLED BY THEIR PARENTS IN PRIVATE SCHOOLS WHEN FAPE IS AT ISSUE

Sec. 300.148 Placement of children by parents when FAPE [free appropriate public education] is at issue.

(a) General. This part does not require an LEA to pay for the cost of education, including special education and related services, of a child with a disability at a private school or facility if that agency made FAPE available to the child and the parents elected to place the child in a private school or facility. However, the public agency must include that child in the population whose needs are addressed consistent with §§ 300.131 through 300.144.

(b) Disagreements about FAPE. Disagreements between the parents and a public agency regarding the availability of a program appropriate for the child, and the question of financial reimbursement, are subject to the due process procedures in §§ 300.504 through 300.520.

(c) Reimbursement for private school placement. If the parents of a child with a disability, who previously received special education and related services under the authority of a public agency, enroll the child in a private preschool, elementary school, or secondary school without the consent of or referral by the public agency, a court or a hearing officer may require the agency to reimburse the parents for the cost of that enrollment if the court or hearing officer finds that the agency had not made FAPE available to the child in a timely manner prior to that enrollment and that the private placement is appropriate. A parental placement may be found to be appropriate by a hearing officer or a court even if it does not meet the State standards that apply to education provided by the SEA and LEAs.

(d) Limitation on reimbursement. The cost of reimbursement described in paragraph (c) of this section may be reduced or denied—

(1) If—

(i) At the most recent IEP Team meeting that the parents attended prior to removal of the child from the public school, the parents did not inform the IEP Team that they were rejecting the placement proposed by the public agency to provide FAPE to their child, including stating their concerns and their intent to enroll their child in a private school at public expense; or

(ii) At least ten (10) business days (including any holidays that occur on a business day) prior to the removal of the child from the public school, the parents did not give written notice to the public agency of the information described in paragraph (d)(1)(i) of this section;

(2) If, prior to the parents' removal of the child from the public school, the public agency informed the parents, through the notice requirements described in § 300.503(a)(1), of its intent to

evaluate the child (including a statement of the purpose of the evaluation that was appropriate and reasonable), but the parents did not make the child available for the evaluation; or

(3) Upon a judicial finding of unreasonableness with respect to actions taken by the parents.

(e) Exception. Notwithstanding the notice requirement in paragraph (d)(1) of this section, the cost of reimbursement—

(1) Must not be reduced or denied for failure to provide the notice if—

(i) The school prevented the parents from providing the notice;

(ii) The parents had not received notice, pursuant to § 300.504, of notice requirement in paragraph (d)(1) of this section; or

(iii) Compliance with paragraph (d)(1) of this section would likely result in physical harm to the child; and

(2) May, in the discretion of the court or a hearing officer, not be reduced or denied for failure to provide this notice if—

(i) The parents are not literate or cannot write in English; or

(ii) Compliance with paragraph (d)(1) of this section would likely result in serious emotional harm to the child. (Authority: 20 U.S.C.A. § 1412(a)(10)(c))

APPENDIX B

USEFUL EDUCATION LAW WEB SITES

Legal Search Engines

http://washlaw.edu	contains law-related sources on the Internet.
http://www.findlaw.com	helps to find any Web site that is law related.
http://www.alllaw.com	contains law-related sources on the Internet.
http://www.law.cornell.edu/	provides research and electronic publishing.

U.S. SUPREME COURT, FEDERAL COURTS, AND FEDERAL GOVERNMENT WEB SITES

www.supremecourtus.gov	official website of the U.S. Supreme Court.
http://supct.law.cornell.edu	useful information on the Supreme Court.
http://thomas.loc.gov/	prepared by the Library of Congress, links to the federal Court System.
www.uscourts.gov	U.S. Federal Judiciary Web site.
www.gpoaccess.gov/fr/index .html	contains the Federal Register.
www.ed.gov	U.S. Department of Education Web site.

http://idea.ed.gov	Department of Education Web site for the IDEA
www.house.gov/	U.S. House of Representatives Web site.
www.senate.gov	U.S. Senate Web site.
www.whitehouse.gov	Web site of the White House.

ABOUT THE AUTHORS

Charles J. Russo, JD, EdD, is the Joseph Panzer Chair in Education in the School of Education and Allied Professions and Adjunct Professor in the School of Law at the University of Dayton, Ohio. He is also an Extra-Ordinary (Visiting) Professor in the Faculty of Education at the Potchefstroom Campus of North-West University in Potchefstroom, South Africa. The 1998–1999 president of the Education Law Association and 2002 recipient of its McGhehey (Lifetime Achievement) Award, he is the author of almost two hundred articles in peer-reviewed journals and the author, coauthor, editor, or coeditor of thirty-four books. He has been the editor of the *Yearbook of Education Law* for the Education Law Association since 1995 and has written or coauthored almost seven hundred publications; he is also the editor of two academic journals and serves as a member of more than a dozen editorial boards. He has spoken and taught extensively on issues in education law in the United States and in twenty-two other nations on all six inhabited continents. In recognition of his work in education law in other countries, he received an honorary PhD from Potchefstroom University, now the Potchefstroom Campus of North-West University, in Potchefstroom, South Africa, in May of 2004. He earned his JD and EdD at St. John's University in his native New York City.

Allan G. Osborne Jr., EdD, is the former principal of the Snug Harbor Community School in Quincy, Massachusetts. Retired after thirty-four years as a special education teacher and school administrator, he is currently serving as an adjunct professor of school law at several colleges and universities. He received his doctorate in educational leadership from Boston College. Allan Osborne has authored or coauthored numerous articles, monographs, textbooks, and textbook chapters on special education law, along with textbooks on other aspects of special education. A past president of the Education Law Association (ELA), he is the 2008 recipient of its McGhehey Award for lifetime achievement and service. He has been a frequent presenter at national school law and special education conferences and writes the "Students with Disabilities" chapter of the *Yearbook of Education Law,* which is published by ELA. He is on the Editorial Advisory Committee of *West's Education Law Reporter* and is coeditor of the "Education Law Into Practice" section of that journal. He also serves as an editorial consultant for many other publications in education law, administration, and special education.

Rev. Joseph D. Massucci, PhD, is an associate professor and chair of the Department of Educational Leadership in the School of Education and Allied Professions at the University of Dayton in Ohio. He has extensive experience as a secondary-school principal and Catholic-school educator at the local, state, and national levels. Rev. Massucci received his master's degree from the Catholic University of America; he earned his Educational Specialist degree and doctorate in educational leadership from the University of Dayton. He has authored and coauthored articles primarily dealing with Catholic schools, urban schools, non-public schools, vouchers, and school management/leadership issues.

Gerald M. Cattaro, EdD, is Professor of Education, Chair of the Division of Educational Leadership Administration and Policy, as well as Director of the Center of Non Public Education and Catholic Leadership in the Graduate School of Education at Fordham University in New York City. He is currently on the editorial board of *Education and Urban Society* and the Governing Board of *Catholic Education: Journal of Inquiry and Research.* He was an administrator in non-public schools in New York City for more than twenty years. He writes and speaks, nationally and internationally, on governance issues associated with non-public schools, executive leadership of non-public schools, non-public school policy, and international non-public education. Dr. Cattaro earned his EdD at Teachers College of Columbia University in New York City.

www.ingramcontent.com/pod-product-compliance
Ingram Content Group UK Ltd.
Pitfield, Milton Keynes, MK11 3LW, UK
UKHW040417181125
465134UK00003BA/441